When you offer a people
tion of leadership in their
hope, and then he leads us well. He teaches us what
Paul preached and Wesley knew, what Churchill
proclaimed and what generations of believers have
lived: that hope is a fuel for our faith, a source of
strength for our mission, and a vital undergirding of
our vision. Thank God for Terry Law.

—STEPHEN MANSFIELD, PHD
NEW YORK TIMES BEST-SELLING AUTHOR

I have known Terry Law for many years and have
always thought of him as a cross between the apostle
Paul and James Bond. When the scriptures mention
the uttermost parts of the earth, you can rest assured
Terry has been there. He has brought hope to
millions around the world, and now—through this
book—he helps you and me find the hope we have
lost or discover the hope we never had.

—JIM STOVALL
AUTHOR, *THE ULTIMATE GIFT*

So many people today have lost sight of the real
hope in the world, and those who do have hope have
had their vision clouded to where they feel they too
have lost hope. People wonder where God is in the
midst of a sin-filled world. Terry Law and Jim Gilbert
present how to have lasting hope, what leads to hope,
and how to learn to choose hope in the midst of what
seem to be hopeless situations.

—RON LUCE
PRESIDENT AND FOUNDER OF
TEEN MANIA MINISTRIES

The HOPE HABIT

TERRY LAW
and
JIM GILBERT

Charisma
HOUSE
A STRANG COMPANY

Most STRANG COMMUNICATIONS BOOK GROUP products are available at special quantity discounts for bulk purchase for sales promotions, premiums, fund-raising, and educational needs. For details, write Strang Communications Book Group, 600 Rinehart Road, Lake Mary, Florida 32746, or telephone (407) 333-0600.

THE HOPE Habit by Terry Law and Jim Gilbert
Published by Charisma House
A Strang Company
600 Rinehart Road
Lake Mary, Florida 32746
www.strangbookgroup.com

Cover design by Justin Evans
Design Director: Bill Johnson

Copyright © 2010 by Terry Law Ministries, Inc.
All rights reserved

Library of Congress Cataloging-in-Publication Data:

Law, Terry.
  The hope habit / by Terry Law and Jim Gilbert. -- 1st ed.
      p. cm.
  Includes bibliographical references (p.   ).
  ISBN 978-1-59979-998-8
  1. Hope--Religious aspects--Christianity. I. Gilbert, Jim. II. Title.
  BV4638.L39 2010
  241'.4--dc22

                                                2010000051

First Edition

10 11 12 13 14 — 9 8 7 6 5 4 3 2 1
Printed in the United States of America

*To my wife, Barbara. Thank you for bringing
me hope when my own was exhausted. May the God
of hope fill us with all joy and peace, that
we may abound in hope always.*
TL

*To my daughter, Alexandria Hope. May my hopes
illuminate your dreams.*
JG

CONTENTS

1

WHATEVER HAPPENED TO HOPE?

No one can live without hope....It is hope
that heals. Hope is the basic energy of civilization, of social existence, of individual
life.[1]

—DAVID AUGSBURGER

WHATEVER HAPPENED TO hope? Where did it go?
The disappearance of hope is easy to explain
in some places. In much of Africa, it has withered
in the shadow of AIDS. In the Islamic world, too many men
"find" it only in suicide, while Muslim women are forbidden
to look for it in the first place. And for India's more than one
hundred sixty million Untouchables, hope seems never to
have existed at all.[2]

Hope is also very hard to find these days in places that
used to brim with it. In 2003, for example, the late Pope John
Paul II called for the church to proclaim "a message of hope
to a Europe that seems to have lost sight of it"[3] and lamented
what he characterized as "grave uncertainties...[in] culture,
anthropology, ethics, and spirituality."[4] The numbers agree
with him: European lack of hope is dramatically illustrated by

what observers describe as "demographic suicide," i.e., fewer and fewer marriages and a rapidly declining population. Birth rates are an especially accurate barometer of national expectations; high birth rates equal high hopes, while low birth rates are a dead giveaway that the future has become unimportant if not bleak. All over Europe, once great cultures malnourished from two centuries of feeding on the plastic fruit of secularism are simply dying off.

Here in the land of plenty, hope seems to have taken a backseat to cynicism. Whether true or not, it is a given in twenty-first century America that CEOs loot their corporations, television evangelists are hypocrites, there are no honest politicians, and everybody cheats in school. From environmentalist fearmongers to doom-and-gloom prophecy pundits, the national spirit is sagging. Dad has twenty years on the job, but he's at a creative dead end, and an impending corporate merger has him worried about being "downsized." At home, Mom is reading a paperback about how recent events in the Middle East are a sign that Armageddon is just around the corner. And little Johnny and his kindergarten playmates have already been saddled with the burden that it's up to them to "save the planet."

Newspapers don't help. Today's coverage is relentlessly bleak.[5] Ditto TV, which beams the world's catastrophes directly into our living rooms in real time. And home computers bring their own bad news—from e-mail scams and chat-room stalkers to pornographic pop-up ads. Mom has to be a full-time security guard.

As I write, Joe Average has lately watched his hopes evaporate along with his retirement account, while Bob Billionaire begs Washington for a bailout. Tens of millions of voters have hitched their wagon to a presidency that cannot possibly prove as messianic as they wish.

In a culture that has abandoned heroes for celebrities, young people pin their hopes on an image in the mirror, an illusive ideal that always needs to shed pounds, get a tan, add a tattoo, erase a wrinkle, or even bend a gender in order for life—or at least next Friday night—to work out right.

> *Here in the land of plenty, hope seems to have taken a backseat to cynicism.*

Where is hope for marriages that often don't last as long as the engagements that preceded them? What about the second or third try? Is there hope in a prenuptial agreement, or is signing one an admission of no hope? Does hope exist for the sensitive young man who has just heard an "expert" tell him he's a woman trapped in a man's body? Does it exist for the young woman at a Christian college who doesn't drink or smoke but spends her nights bingeing and purging and cutting her own skin?

Is there hope for *you*?

"I don't know who to believe," you might have told yourself.

"If I were gone tomorrow, nobody would notice. My life doesn't count for anything."

"I'll never get out of debt in an economy this bad."

"Society's problems are overwhelming. There's no way I can make a difference."

"What's the use of praying? There's just no hope for me."

THE REASON WHY

We can blame the economy, a host of neuroses, or general moral decay, but there is one underlying reason why so many people near and far have lost hope: *the group of people most responsible for offering hope to the world has failed to display it.* Self-professed followers of Jesus have stood up for morality and traditional values, but they have done so with an overall air of joyless sobriety. Author and researcher David Kinnaman describes Americans' wholesale shift *away* from the Christian faith since 1996, especially on the part of sixteen- to twenty-nine-year olds, a group he dubs "outsiders."

> One crucial insight kept popping up in our exploration. In studying thousands of outsiders' impressions, it is clear that Christians are primarily perceived for what they stand against. *We have become famous for what we oppose rather than who we are for....* In our national surveys we found the three most common perceptions of present-day Christianity are anti-homosexual (an image held by 91 percent of young outsiders), judgmental (87 percent), and hypocritical (85 percent). These "big three" are followed by the following negative perceptions embraced by a majority of young adults: old-fashioned, too involved in politics, out of touch with reality, insensitive to others, boring, not accepting of other faiths, and confusing. When they think of the Christian faith, these are the images that come to mind. This is what a new generation really thinks about Christianity.[6]

Thousands of churches and related ministries have dedicated billions of dollars to reach America's youth with the gospel, yet young people still think of Christians as intolerant and Jesus Himself as nothing more than a great teacher. How could they have arrived at such warped conclusions? I believe it is because, for at least a century now, we have preached a "pie in the sky" kind of hope instead of one based on the life-transforming, culture-redeeming gospel of the Son of God. We have primarily told the world that if they give their lives to Jesus, they'll go to heaven when they die. "Just say this prayer after me. That's all there is to it."

> *There is one underlying reason why so many people near and far have lost hope: the group of people most responsible for offering hope to the world has failed to display it.*

Fine. Now they're ready for eternity, but what about next Monday morning? What about the job market, marriage, and sick kids, not to mention weightier matters ranging from terrorism to human trafficking? *By offering salvation primarily as a ticket to heaven we have implied, not too subtly, that there's not much hope for here and now.*

If, as Pastor Rick Warren says, "life on earth is just the dress rehearsal before the real production,"[7] then shouldn't Christians, more than anyone else, be known as the most hopeful people in this world? I mean really hopeful—not disengaged homebodies always dreaming of what heaven will be like—but dependable, joyful followers of Jesus, renowned for coming up with workable solutions in a broken society.

Hope should be our calling card, the first thing people think of when they see us. Yet the sad reality among today's Christians is that hope, like the late comedian Rodney Dangerfield, "don't get no respect." Fatalism has taken its place.

FATALISM

You remember Murphy's Law, don't you? "If anything can go wrong, it will." When my musical missions teams[8] used to travel into the USSR, things went haywire so often that you would have thought Murphy's Law was the basis for the Soviet constitution. These days, for millions of Western Christians, such pessimism is increasingly becoming a mind-set.

When pessimism becomes a habit it's called *fatalism*. Pessimism is Satan's tool of discouragement, but fatalism is his goal. He wants you to give up on hope so that he can lead you so far into a desert of despair that you're left spiritually blind, deaf, and dumb—in a word: dead. Author David Augsburger describes the onset of a fatalistic mind-set this way:

> A sense of impossibility overwhelms the soul.... [Then] a feeling of immensity overshadows everything....A conviction of futility permeates all thought....A mood of apathy descends over the whole self. (Who cares; so why should I care?)
>
> Impossibility, immensity, futility, and apathy interlock to create a deep sense of helplessness. Whether these are attitudes learned in one's family of origin or modeled by significant people in one's life, they can well up in times of difficulty to silence the voice of hope within and without.[9]

Fatalism is part and parcel of many of the world's so-called "great" religions. Buddhism, for example, is based upon the idea that the essence of life is suffering and that freedom from suffering is *nirvana*, a word that suggests extinguishment of not only the candle of life but also wax, wick, ash, and air, down to the last atom of energy. In other words, Buddhism aspires to absolute nothingness—not happiness, not life, just nonexistence.

Islam is just as fatalistic, but whereas Buddhism starves the soul, Islam is a cancer that devours it. Is it anything less than fatalism that a Muslim's only guarantee of heaven is to commit suicide in the act of killing infidels?

Hinduism, the religion of yet another billion people, has even institutionalized fatalism. It teaches that your present station in life is the wage, good or bad, from previous incarnations. In other words, not only does life stink, but also you deserve it. While good deeds might pay off with higher status in the next life, it is utterly wrong to try to improve your lot in this one.

Then there's Christianity—yes, Christianity! I'm not talking about the "faith which was once for all delivered to the saints" (Jude 3, NKJV) but the twisted, unbiblical mentality that moans, "God is in control; there's nothing I can do." Where, from Adam's sin to John's revelation, is such hopelessness justified in Scripture? *Nowhere!* Instead, fatalism among Christians is fed largely by the gloomy scenario so prevalent in contemporary teaching on the End Times and by the age-old controversy over God's sovereignty versus man's responsibility.

In the first case, Jesus's Great Commission[10] to go and make disciples of the nations is nullified by a Chicken Little mind-set that abandons hope in favor of plans for escape. This attitude trades the gospel of occupation for one of evacuation. The result is a shallow, salt-free message that might make a few timid converts but will never change nations.

In the latter case, the same Great Commission is rendered completely pointless. If God has predestined a "chosen few" for salvation, then why waste time preaching to those *not* chosen? In both scenarios, individual believers are robbed of hope and the church is immobilized in its mission.

Famed Bible smuggler Brother Andrew insists that "we can no longer tolerate [Christian fatalism]. We must fight it for all we are worth, because it is the most powerful weapon the enemy is using at this point in history to defeat the purposes of God."[11]

Is Brother Andrew right? Are we at war with an enemy? Yes, says theologian J. I. Packer.

> I think you know that evil is abroad in God's world: cunning, malicious, destructive evil, resourceful and implacable, headed up by a corrupted angel whom Scripture calls Satan (a Hebrew word meaning "the adversary" or "hostile opponent"). I think you know that Satan is here and now pursuing you personally, since by committing yourself to Jesus Christ you have lined up against him. By walking into the ongoing conflict between the Creator and the corrupter, which you did when you enlisted on the Lord's side, you have ensured that, willy-nilly, you will be living the rest of your life in a state of spiritual warfare. I think you know that not having managed to keep you from faith, Satan will do his [best] to keep you from healthy growth in Christ and usefulness to him in work and witness.[12]

The two most telltale indicators of fatalism in today's Western church are *prayerlessness* and *anemic giving*. Beyond saying grace at mealtime, Western Christians generally neither pray nor pay the tithe.[13] In fact, the most reliable research indicates that "less than one out of every ten" Christians tithes.[14]

But then, why should they? Why give 10 percent of your

income when the church appears to be making less and less impact on society? Why give to missions work if "prophecy" makes it clear that most of the world is going to reject the gospel? Why pray for healing or lost souls when God has already decided everything ahead of time? *Why get your hopes up when it won't make a difference anyway?*

> *The two most telltale indicators of fatalism in today's Western church are prayerlessness and anemic giving.*

Professor Peter Wagner recalls that he was "taught in seminary that the most important function of prayer was to change me and mold me. God never changes. He is sovereign and He will do what he intends to do whether I pray or not."[15] How discouraging! Wagner later learned that this was an extreme, unbalanced form of Calvinism (the theology originated by the sixteenth-century French reformer John Calvin). In his book *Churches That Pray*, he called upon a Calvinist friend, Alvin Vander Griend, for a balanced perspective.

> God wants to be asked not because He is powerless but because of the way He has chosen to exercise His will. We are not pawns on a giant chessboard. We are involved. Only a cold, hard, mechanistic view of God's sovereignty and predestination assumes that God discounts our prayer and simply moves in accord with a predetermined, once-for-all plan. This is not a biblical view of God; it resembles a fatalistic, Muslim-like view of sovereignty that the Bible repudiates.[16]

God can do whatever He wants, but He doesn't want to do it without us! Why? Because God is a *father.* Calvinist teaching, for all its profound insight into divine sovereignty, tends to overlook the fact that God presents Himself to man primarily as a loving father rather than a transcendent sovereign. Of course He is both, but by sending us His Son, He has chosen to reveal Himself as Father *more than anything else.* That is why all of Jesus's recorded prayers in Scripture, save one, start with the Son calling on His Father.

> *This book is all about hope as a mind-set, a habitual choice. In other words, whether you are hopeful or hopeless is up to you.*

"Ask a Muslim, 'Who is God?'" says Brother Andrew, "and he'll answer by reciting a list of ninety-nine attributes of God—not one of which is *Father*."[17]

Father and *son* are family terms connoting inclusion and intimacy, and thanks to the regenerating power of the Holy Spirit, they can include you and me. Even better, the Bible says that along with being God's children, we are "joint heirs" with Christ.[18]

Now, how can an heir of the Most High God *not* brim with hope? Yes, there are daily discouragements to face, and they will continue as long as we're caught in time's "mortal coil." But remember, we're talking about a *mind-set*, a general outlook, rather than a momentary emotion. In this light, pessimism isn't just a bad habit; it is a denial of true Christian faith.

This book is all about hope as a mind-set, a habitual choice, the course of *first* resort when despair tries an ambush. In other words, whether you are hopeful or hopeless is up to *you.*

A WORLD OF CHOICES

You might feel like you don't have many choices in life, but the truth is you are constantly making them. In this world of sensory overload you are forced to make choices all day, every day, as TV networks, radio pitchmen, flashing neon signs, "urgent" e-mails, sweepstakes junk-mailers, and even cereal box inserts compete for your attention. On any given day you are bombarded with more words and pictures than your great-grandfather encountered in a year. You *must* make choices, decide which clamoring voices will have your ear—your money—and then filter out the rest. On the one hand you can watch an American president being sworn into office as television beams living history into your living room. On the other you can banish reality by flipping the channel to the unvarnished vulgarity of MTV and let yourself turn into what one commentator calls a "videot." Yes, you have choices.

Management guru Peter Drucker believes choice is the defining feature of our age.

> In a few hundred years, when the history of our time is written from a long-term perspective, it is likely that the most important event those historians will see is not technology, not the Internet, not e-commerce. It is an unprecedented change in the human condition. For the first time—literally—substantial and rapidly growing numbers of people have choices. For the first time, they will have to manage themselves.
>
> And society is totally unprepared for it.[19]

We often must make choices quickly, in those moments when fact collides with feeling. For example, imagine you are piloting a small airplane and you find yourself in the middle of a blinding snowstorm. Your check your instruments and are surprised that they show you banking hard right, gaining altitude, and about to stall. That can't be true, you tell yourself, because everything "feels" level to you. Which will you choose to believe, your inner ear or those gauges you paid so much for? Obviously, trusting the gauges is the smart choice, especially if you don't want it to be the last one you ever make. Yet too many fliers, when facing that scenario, have let their feelings lead them to their deaths.

> *"For the first time...people have choices. For the first time, they will have to manage themselves. And society is totally unprepared for it." —Peter Drucker*

Maybe you're caught in a similar situation. Your life is in a nosedive, and your vision is so clouded by poor advice and bad habits that you don't see the ground coming up at you. If that describes you, then think of *The Hope Habit* as a set of gauges, easy-to-read principles from God's Word that will guide you not just to safety but also to where you really want your life to go. These pages will present you with clear choices, intelligent, life-saving alternatives to the flawed thinking and fatalistic habits that got you into your current tailspin. For example, I want to help you:

- "Hope in the LORD; for with the LORD there is lovingkindness, and with Him is abundant redemption" (Psalm 130:7).
- Know that "surely there is a future, and your hope will not be cut off" (Proverbs 23:18).
- Be assured that God has "plans to take care of you, not abandon you, plans to give you

the future you hope for" (Jeremiah 29:11, THE MESSAGE).

- Be filled "with all joy and peace in believing, so that you will abound in hope by the power of the Holy Spirit" (Romans 15:13).
- "Continue in the faith firmly established and steadfast, and not moved away from the hope of the gospel that you have heard" (Colossians 1:23).
- Learn to wear "the breastplate of faith and love, and as a helmet, the hope of salvation" (1 Thessalonians 5:8).
- Learn to "hold fast [your] confidence and the boast of [your] hope firm until the end" (Hebrews 3:6).
- "Have strong encouragement to take hold of the hope set before [you]...as an anchor of the soul, a hope both sure and steadfast" (Hebrews 6:18–19).
- Know that you have been "born again to a living hope through the resurrection of Jesus Christ from the dead" (1 Peter 1:3).
- "Fix your hope completely on the grace to be brought to you at the revelation of Jesus Christ" (1 Peter 1:13).

Even in the worst, most intractable circumstances, there is hope for you if you're willing to choose it. Maybe you don't believe me right now. You might be saying that if I knew what you're up against, I would understand. But keep reading. You'll see that your circumstances—your whole life—can change.

THE PARADIGM OF HOPE

Your paradigm is your way of looking at the world, not consciously but unconsciously. It is the set of assumptions you use as a starting point every day, the multitude of "facts" you rely upon without a second (or even first) thought: Gravity will hold me down. My chair will hold me. Food will nourish my body. I'll get paid for working. Most people inherit their paradigms from their parents, teachers, and peers. That is why, for example, a recent presidential straw poll conducted among elementary students at a private Florida school yielded "results" nearly identical to their parents' actual votes.

Once in a while you might undergo a paradigm *shift*, an adjustment you're forced to make because something you took for granted suddenly changed. For example, my coauthor Jim Gilbert once walked onstage in front of an audience of a thousand people and started to take his seat at the piano. He didn't question the reliability of the bench because he always sat on benches and they always held him...until this time. "The bench splintered into a hundred pieces, and I found myself sprawled on the floor," he remembers with a chuckle. "Band members and audience alike were howling with laughter, so I just stood up, took a bow, and played standing up until someone brought me a chair. But for the next three years, I *never* sat down at a piano without checking the bench."

Jim experienced—quite literally—a paradigm shift. Something he had always automatically relied on was now unreliable. Regarding chairs, he had to adopt a new way of thinking.

> *Hope is the confident expectation of the goodness of God.*

If you have become fatalistic, if you feel trapped by your circumstances and can't see a way out, then I want to show you a new paradigm—the paradigm of hope, which I briefly define as *the confident expectation of the goodness of God.*[20] Other sources are more comprehensive. Noah Webster's 1828 dictionary defines *hope* as "confidence in a future event; the highest degree of well-founded expectation of good; as a hope founded on God's gracious promises; a scriptural sense." Likewise, *Vine's Complete Expository Dictionary of Old and New Testament Words* describes *hope* as "favourable and confident expectation; the happy anticipation of good, the object of which is God."[21]

This kind of hope will precipitate a fundamental shift in your thinking, deep down at the level of your mental reflexes. But I assure you; it will be worth it. *It is my firm conviction that you can live a life—a lifestyle—of hope.* This is not cheap optimism, a pep talk sprinkled with Bible references. Any of my friends can tell you that I'm not one to see the world through rose-colored glasses. I'm talking about real hope, the kind that knows "God causes all things to work together for good to those who love God, to those who are called according to His purpose."[22]

How the Almighty accomplishes this might surprise you. "We exult in our troubles," said St. Paul, because troubles develop "perseverance; and perseverance, proven character, and proven character, hope."[23] It might seem like a convoluted idea that life's troubles are the beginning of hope. "Wait a minute," you say to yourself. "That's certainly not *my* experience. I've seen plenty of trouble, and it hasn't produced anything in me but the opposite of hope."

That may be true, but realize that Paul was speaking about the *right* response to tribulation, not just a gut reaction. And that is the central theme of this book: *hope is a choice, not a feeling.* Like love, it is more verb than noun, more deliberate than impulsive.

Perhaps you think it's too late for you to make such a shift in your thinking, that "you can't teach an old dog new tricks." But you're wrong! You are a person, not a "higher" animal, and you were created in the image of a God who dearly loves you. No matter how many years may have slipped through your fingers, thanks to God's grace and mercy, every minute of your future is still on your side. It's a matter of choice, not fate.

I know this for one simple reason: *there is no such thing as fate!* It is a pagan concept whose meaning is derived from the same root as the word *fatal*, and it stands in total contradiction to the existence of a providential God. Just as fear can lead to greater fear, believing in fate is ultimately fatal. God, on the other hand, "has not given [you] a spirit of fear, but of power and of love and of a sound mind."[24] He has something so much better for you.

> *Hope is a choice, not a feeling. Like love,*
> *it is more verb than noun, more deliberate*
> *than impulsive.*

Rewrite Your Obituary

On August 27, 2008, the Bloomberg financial newswire erroneously announced the death of Steve Jobs, the celebrated CEO of Apple, Inc., maker of the Macintosh computer, the iPod, and the iPhone. Bloomberg quickly retracted the error, and the very-much-alive Jobs took the gaffe in good-humored stride. But Wall Street shuddered nevertheless, since analysts estimated at the time that the departure of Jobs from the company for any reason would have devalued Apple's stock by twenty-five billion dollars.

More than a century earlier a French typesetter made a

similar mistake that spread like a virus throughout the world's newspapers, going uncorrected for weeks. "The Merchant of Death Is Dead!" screamed that first headline about Alfred Nobel, the Swedish chemist whose invention of dynamite the editors obviously had opposed. In reality, Alfred's oil-baron brother, Ludvig Nobel, had died, and Alfred, already grieving at his loss, now had to endure one editorial condemnation after another as the error ricocheted around the world. Worse still, many of the articles blamed not only his invention but also Alfred himself for the deaths of millions of people. And even those who were respectful still associated his name in one way or another with death.

Nobel was understandably grieved, but he also realized that being able to read his own obituary presented him with a golden opportunity. He still had time to make his name memorable for something more honorable than death. He could, in effect, rewrite his own obituary.

Alfred succeeded. Today, everyone recognizes him as the originator of the Nobel Prize, which is awarded for achievements in physics, chemistry, physiology, medicine, literature, and most famously, peace.[25] A testament to his success is the fact that many of my readers are doubtless surprised to learn that Alfred Nobel invented dynamite!

Now, what if you could also rewrite *your* obituary? What if you could leave the dead-end life you think you deserve and head straight into the destiny you think you've lost? The fact is, you can, because you have the God-given power to choose hope. It may be the only power you have left in life, but it is yours; no one can take it from you.

Here is your first choice: You can put down this book and say, "I don't want to go there." Or you can read on and discover the power of hope.

Hope mobilizes.
It puts together
  a disciplined surge
  toward the crack
  in the door of the future.
And the remarkable thing
  is that time and time again
  the door yields
  to a determined push.
Hope springs locks
  as surely as calling a situation
  "a hopeless case"
  fulfills its own prophecies.[26]

2

THE MEANING OF HOPE

Hope is patience with the lamp lit.
                              —TERTULLIAN

How many books have you seen or sermons have you heard about hope? Faith and love have been extolled so frequently in our generation that they comprise whole sections in religious bookstores, yet hope gets short shrift. Tell a friend you're hoping for a good result, and you'll often get a look that says, "I feel sorry for you." You might even receive an exhortation to "have faith," as though hope were mere wishful thinking rather than the revealing of the greatest mystery in the history of the world: "Christ in you, the hope of glory."[1]

Hope is an *abiding* virtue, meaning there is something permanent, something *eternal* about it. "But now faith, hope, love, abide these three; but the greatest of these is love," is the way St. Paul put it.[2] Plenty of preachers have encouraged their listeners to build up their faith and to grow in love. But it is equally important for you to understand that *God requires that you build your hope as well.* That is what Paul encouraged the Roman believers to do: "Now may the God of hope fill you with all joy and peace in believing, so that you will abound in hope by the power of the Holy Spirit."[3]

WHAT IS HOPE?

Hope is a dynamic spiritual force that the Bible likens both to a helmet,[4] because it protects the mind, and an anchor,[5] because it keeps you steady when life gets rough. But in simplest terms, as I defined it earlier, hope is *a confident expectation of the goodness of God.*

> *Plenty of preachers have encouraged their listeners to build up their faith and to grow in love. But it is equally important for you to understand that God requires that you build your hope as well.*

The late educator and TV evangelist Oral Roberts always personified that definition better than most, as evidenced by his signature opening line: "Something *good* is going to *happen* to *you!*" Those were the first eight words out of his mouth every time he made a public appearance, and sometimes he both opened *and* closed his television broadcast with them. Roberts wasn't simply trying to set a positive tone. He knew down in his depths that God is a good God and that nothing else about Him can really sink in until that truth does. He understood the unique, foundational nature of hope.

True hope is hinged upon the one historical fact that is unique to Christianity: Jesus's resurrection. Every other religion depends upon its founder's teachings or laws, but according to St. Paul, "If Christ has not been raised, then our preaching is vain, [and] your faith also is vain."[6] Christianity stands or falls on whether or not Jesus is risen from the dead.

The world's major non-Christian religions, by contrast,

constantly illustrate how futile they are by the hopelessness they have bred in their billions of followers. I've seen it first-hand in the anguished rage of young Muslim men who think committing mass murder is their only chance for salvation. I've seen it in the blank stares of malnourished Hindu children whose parents have taught them that perpetual hunger is their fate, a destiny there's no point in trying to overcome.

I have seen hopelessness for decades in the faces of disillusioned atheists, from Russia to China, who understand Paul's point instinctively—even though most have never read the Bible—that *no God means no hope*. Marx, Lenin, and later Chairman Mao tried to substitute hope with a promise that their brand of revolution would bring a people's paradise. Yet rarely in history has any promise failed more spectacularly than the false hope of communism.

IN THE MIRROR

My closest encounter with hopelessness, however, came not in Iraq or India, nor did it come behind an iron or bamboo curtain, but it came on the scene of my life's biggest battle: at home.

I had always been what you might call a natural optimist. While others were contemplating whether the glass was half full or half empty, I was the kid off somewhere looking for a bigger glass! Such a disposition is not really "natural," of course. It is the gift of God to equip me for my calling. I've had some hard assignments over the past four decades, from encounters with the Soviet secret police during Eastern Europe's communist era to dodging al Qaeda's assassination plots in Iraq. The Lord has worked a certain toughness into me so that I am not easily discouraged.

But optimism isn't hope, and it certainly doesn't make a man invincible. I know, because I've taken a couple of spiritual body blows over the years that almost knocked me out for good. The death of my first wife, Jan, was one of them. She was just thirty-five years old when an auto accident took her life, and with it the hearts of a husband and three children. Jan was half Norwegian, half Italian, and all sunshine, her beautiful olive complexion framing a dazzling smile. She had a heart as big as the world and never complained at having to share me with it, taking our frequent separations in gentle stride as one of the sacrifices to be made in our calling together.

Our greatest treasures often are those we cannot value until they're stripped from us. Send a rich man off to Alcatraz, and you'll find that it's not his country club or big cars that he misses, but those everyday blessings so often overlooked—a favorite coffee mug, the smell of grass after a rain shower, waking to his wife's smile in the morning. So it was with Jan. She was a necessity of life whose enormous worth I could not fully appreciate until she was taken from me. My soul was impoverished without her. In the months that followed her death I plunged into an abyss of despair. I couldn't work, couldn't sleep, and couldn't think clearly or even pray. Nighttime was worst, and often I would just drive the two-lane roads south of Tulsa until the sun came up.

> *True hope is hinged upon the one historical fact that is unique to Christianity: Jesus's resurrection.*

My eventual emergence from that dark time came through discovering the power of praise and worship,[7] a catharsis so liberating that it reshaped not merely my preaching but my entire paradigm for ministry around the world. I learned what it meant to be God's instrument to give people "beauty for ashes, the oil of joy for mourning, the garment of praise for the spirit of heaviness,"[8] because He had done precisely that for me.

In time I remarried and went from being the father of three to the father of six wonderful children. Overseas, nation after nation opened to my ministry, especially after the collapse of the Soviet Union, where I had labored in the Christian underground for so long. On the home front, my books on praise and worship were becoming best sellers, and, more importantly, appeared catalytic in launching a whole new generation of worshipers. Life was so wonderful for a while that I would have needed oxygen to fly any higher.

Of course, everyone encounters valleys between the mountaintops, and eventually challenges arose in my second marriage. But I loved my wife—all the more after my previous loss—and was doggedly determined that the two of us would know nothing short of complete spiritual victory in our union. If God could bring down iron curtains, surely He could *and would* tear down the barriers that Satan tried to raise between us.

Then came the second blow.

After eleven years of marriage, and having exhausted every spiritual resource, I found myself being served papers of divorce. The shock, the pain, the shame—they were utterly indescribable. Years earlier I had survived a marriage cut short by death, coming through it with my faith in God renewed and my ministry strengthened. But how do you survive divorce?

Far from strengthening one's ministry, divorce can shatter it. No matter who is to blame, it is the tattoo of failure, a permanent stain on one's reputation. Death brings widowhood, but divorce is a ticket to exile. Friendships once presumed secure suddenly cease, smaller divorces in their own right, like aftershocks trailing a big quake.

I had been a faithful husband and tried my best, yet I still felt disqualified from the ministry and in weaker moments considered quitting. But of course I did not quit, whether from godly faithfulness or sheer stubbornness. Furthermore, I practiced what I had learned years earlier, offering sacrifices of thanksgiving and praise down in the "belly" of despair.[9] And once again God was faithful to deliver me.

Nevertheless, in the years since then I have found myself, on more mornings than not, awakening to a sense of impending doom. I have resisted it, of course, but it is still there, a spirit of foreboding that presents itself as often as the sunrise.

Spiritual strongholds, as I have written elsewhere, are not always demonic.[10] They are often thought patterns, mental habits formed by a set of influences (e.g., ingrained family attitudes) or by a series of similar experiences. In my case a number of hardships took its toll on my mind and spirit: accidents both on foreign roads and domestic ski slopes that stole my spirit of adventure, a Yugoslavian train wreck caused by sabotage, the imprisonment of cherished Christian co-workers in the USSR, various direct threats from terrorists and hostile governments. These events, combined with the tragedies of sudden death and humiliating divorce, caused me to develop *an expectation of bad news.* Like a wobbly boxer awaiting the knockout punch, I subconsciously began to brace myself, on a daily basis, for the next attack.

I had always expected that faith, a good confession, and a song of praise would bring me through, and on any given day they certainly did. But like Israel gathering manna in the wilderness, I had no reserve, and I found myself *starting from scratch every morning.* There was no sense of progress, no seizing the day. Instead, suffering lurked just around the corner, *every* corner.

I was battling chronic depression, which the American Medical Association classifies as a disease. According to recent statistics, more than three million Americans suffer from chronic depression,[11] with more than twenty million experiencing related mood disorders.[12] Additionally, depression reaches far beyond the mind and emotions. It weakens the human immune system, thereby worsening a host of physical diseases and contributing to countless premature deaths. In fact, the World Health Organization predicts that depression will be the second largest killer after heart disease by 2020.[13]

I faced depression—and its dead end, despair—after Jan died, and I ultimately conquered it, partly because the choice before me was so black and white: I either had to praise God and resume living or simply give up and start dying, so I chose life.[14] But several years and multiple crises later, that same spirit of heaviness, like clouds that gradually turn a bright morning into a dreary afternoon, subtly crept back in. I really didn't notice it until my soul had become thoroughly soaked in light-obscuring gray.

Beloved British Bible teacher Derek Prince revealed late in his life that he had fought against depression since childhood, a period he called his "gray streak."[15] Another distinguished Briton, Prime Minister Winston Churchill, suffered from severe depression for so many years that he spoke of it as an unwelcome companion, calling it "my black dog." His bouts were so severe at times that he wrote, "I don't like standing near the edge of a platform when an express train is passing through. I like to stand right back and if possible get a pillar between me and the train. I don't like to stand by the side of a ship and look down into the water. A second's action would end everything. A few drops of desperation."[16]

The good news is that Christ in us is "greater than…he who is in the world,"[17] so that "in all these things we are more than conquerors through Him who loved us."[18] Yet the knowledge that we are more than conquerors is useless if we do not learn to *think* and *act* like conquerors.

At this point you might expect a lesson on exercising faith, but that is only part of the equation. Faith is doubtless necessary, but it has to do with the heart more than the head. When it comes to establishing new ways of thinking, faith cannot move its mountains until *hope* shows it how.

THE CERTAINTY OF HOPE

Most people think hope includes at least a shred of uncertainty, while only faith is sure of the outcome. But that is like saying the person who looks both ways before crossing the street is a worrier. Assessing the situation is a sign of good sense, not worry. Hope sees reality and deals with it. "In this way, it is different from blind optimism," says the chief of experimental medicine at Boston's Beth Israel Deaconess Medical Center, Dr. Jerome Groopman.

> It brings reality into sharp focus. In the setting of illness, hope helps us weigh highly charged and often frightening information about the malady and its therapies. Hope incorporates fear into the process of rational deliberation and tempers it so we can think and choose without panic. On the other hand, unbridled fear overwhelms initial hope like a tidal wave, blocking the cognitive intake of information and washing away other feelings.... Hope, then, is the ballast that keeps us steady, that recognizes where along the path are the dangers and pitfalls that can throw us off; hope tempers fear so we can recognize dangers and then bypass or endure them.[19]

At the other end of the continent, in Vancouver, Canada, British-born theologian J. I. Packer also contrasts hope with optimism.

> Optimism is a wish without a warrant; Christian hope is a certainty, guaranteed by God himself. Optimism reflects ignorance as to whether good things will ever actually come. Christian hope expresses knowledge that each day of his life, and every moment beyond it, the believer can say with truth, on the basis of God's own commitment, that the best is yet to come.[20]

True hope, then, is certain of God's goodness and sees reality in light of it. It isn't naïve anymore than faith is blind. To the contrary, hope gives faith its sight.

FAITH AND HOPE

Faith and hope are *symbiotic*; i.e., neither can exist without the other. They are also *synergistic*, working more effectively together than they could separately. In fact, hope without faith is wishful thinking. Yet while faith and hope are interdependent, they are also distinctly different from one another in at least two ways.

Hope sees reality and deals with it.

First, faith resides in the heart, while hope exists in the mind. According to the Bible, faith and love are a breastplate,[21] i.e., they protect the heart, while hope is a *helmet*, guarding the mind.

Concerning faith, the apostle Paul says, "For with the heart a person believes, resulting in righteousness,"[22] while hope comes "through perseverance and the encouragement of the Scriptures."[23] In other words, hope is developed through a combination of teaching and testing (which taken together are the proof of learning).

Second, faith focuses on the present, while hope dares to imagine the future. Many people think they have faith simply because they know God answers prayer. In fact, they "know that I know that I know that God will heal me." But mental assent to the truth is not faith, because faith dwells in the heart and takes action now, while hope dwells in the mind and looks to the future.

Knowing that God *will* heal me is hope, not faith. And that's fine, because there is nothing wrong with hoping to be healed. Yet, as the late Derek Prince warned, "a person who merely accepts truth with his intellect can remain unchanged by it."[24] True hope is eventually authenticated by faith just as surely as tomorrow eventually becomes today.

> *Hope sees the result before faith substantiates it. It is patience with binoculars.*

Hope is oriented toward an imperishable inheritance reserved in heaven. It is the *then* to faith's *now*. And in a world where everyone wants it—and often gets it—*now*, it's easy to understand why faith is more fashionable than hope. This is especially true in evangelical circles where, in church as in business, we've been taught to expect—to *respect*—results.

There's nothing wrong with expecting results, of course, but God's Word teaches us to celebrate our future while we patiently wait for it. And that's where hope comes in. Hope *sees* the result before faith substantiates it. It is patience with binoculars.

Hope is like the architect who can look at mere blue lines on paper and see a building. Faith, on the other hand, is the contractor who takes hope's vision and executes it. Without hope and faith working together, the building won't get built.

In ancient Israel, Jacob's son Joseph had a dream that symbolically but plainly pointed to his future power and prosperity.[25] Although he didn't fully understand it at the time, the young teenager's dream instilled in him an abiding hope. From then on he knew God had a destiny for him to fulfill.

What God did *not* show Joseph in the dream, however, was the rocky path his journey to greatness would take. The young man would, in short order, be assaulted by his own brothers and then sold into a life of slavery in Egypt. In years to come, he would temporarily prosper, only to be wrongly accused of rape and thrown into prison for some thirteen years. Eventually, however, he would rise to the loftiest of Egypt's heights, surpassed in wealth and power only by Pharaoh himself, to whom he became chief advisor.

What kept Joseph going all those years? What enabled him to walk such a difficult path? It was the dream. Joseph's *dream* enabled his *walk*, and his *walk* fulfilled his *dream*. In other words, Joseph made history because his hope and faith worked together, both of them motivated by an all-encompassing love for God.

Getting Started

American civil rights leader Jesse Jackson is famous for exhorting his followers to "keep hope alive." But how do you do that? How can a person break out of a lifetime habit of expecting bad things? My coauthor, Jim Gilbert, laughs a little sadly when he remembers how one young team member from our early days of ministry tried to overcome his penchant for negative thinking.

"He came to me one day to say that the Lord had chastised him for 'always being so negative.' I replied that it seemed unlikely that God would rebuke negativity with yet more negativity. But he never got the point, and thirty-five years later he still doesn't."

Breaking a bad habit isn't simply a matter of stopping it. When a thief stops stealing, he is merely a thief who isn't currently stealing. He must become an honest worker, a contributor to society, before he is truly no longer a thief. Likewise you cannot simply *stop* being depressed; you have to *start* being something else. That means adopting new habits of thought and new responses to the old stimuli that for so long triggered depression. This is where God's Word is absolutely indispensable, and it is exactly why you "have received, not the spirit of the world, but the Spirit who is from God, so that we may know the things freely given to us by God, which things we also speak, not in words taught by human wisdom, but in those taught by the Spirit, combining spiritual thoughts with spiritual words.... [W]e have the mind of Christ."[26]

SAYING, TEACHING, DOING

I pointed out earlier that God has given you a helmet of hope to protect your mind. (See chapter 9 for an in-depth treatment of this subject.) You must not leave this helmet lying on the table; you have to wear it or it is useless. Furthermore, a helmet cannot be worn anywhere else on the body but the head. God designed hope specifically for the mind. Therefore, *putting on the helmet of hope means putting something into your mind.* That something is God's Word.

Veteran soldiers don't need to be reminded to put on their helmets. To the contrary, they train so rigorously that their gear becomes a second skin. In the same way, I endeavor to put on the helmet of hope every morning, just as surely as I shower and shave. I *say* God's Word with my mouth until I know my mind is secured by it. I am not properly ready for the day without this exercise, so I try to be as systematic about it as I am in getting dressed.

I also *teach* others what I learn—no, let me put it differently: I learn even more by teaching others. In fact, one reason we professional talkers record ourselves is because God graciously gives us some of our best, most insightful points while we're speaking.

> *I endeavor to put on the helmet of hope every morning, just as surely as I shower and shave.*

Teaching others what I study also motivates me to *practice* what I preach. Author Stephen Covey says:

> When you teach or share what you're learning with others, you implicitly commit socially to live what you teach. You will naturally be more motivated to live what you're learning. This sharing will be a basis for deepening learning, commitment, and motivation, making change legitimate, and enrolling a support team. You will also find that sharing creates bonding with people—especially with your children. Have them regularly teach you what they are learning in

school. My wife, Sandra, and I have found that doing this simple thing essentially eliminates any need for external motivation with their studies. Those who teach what they are learning are, by far, the greatest students.[27]

Covey's advice fits squarely with the Scripture verse that says we should be "doers of the word, and not merely hearers who delude themselves."[28] Explaining what you are learning to someone else enables you to organize your thoughts and clarify important principles, with the end result that your own understanding is enhanced.

Saying, teaching, and *doing* what God's Word says about you will bring about the paradigm shift we mentioned earlier. Therefore I encourage you to regularly share with others what you learn from these pages. Invite your spouse, children, friends, and co-workers not only to listen but also to discuss encouraging insights with you and to help you adopt new ways of thinking and responding in your everyday living.

Putting on the helmet of hope will enable you to see the world through the eyes of your Creator rather than through the distorted lens of an unrenewed mind. But this is no virtual reality game—it's real! You are about to adopt the very mind-set of the "God of hope."[29]

THE INVITATION TO HOPE

Hope is the word which God has written
on the brow of every man.[1]

—VICTOR HUGO

God HAS WOVEN the ability to hope into every human heart, and it begins to show itself even before we have the vocabulary to express it. Babies hope to walk, so they keep getting up despite falling. Toddlers hope to run, so they keep grinning and lunging forward despite bruised noggins. Children hope to ride on two wheels, so they keep getting back onto their bikes despite scraped knees. Astronauts hope for new space discoveries, so they keep strapping themselves atop rockets despite the risk of a fiery death.

The heights of hope, like the depths of love, can only be fully realized in knowing Christ. But this is not to say that non-Christians do not hope. To the contrary, people everywhere and of all stripes greet each day with some degree of it. "Hoping is the main business of the human spirit," wrote the late Lewis Smedes.[2] Hope propels athletes to break records, spurs suitors to pursue their beloved, and motivates scientists to find cures for diseases. The alarm clock may stir us, but hope gets us out of bed. What else *could* rouse us but the possibility, however remote, that today might turn out to be better than yesterday? Despair would just pull the covers over its head and stay put, but hope—even the faintest flicker of it—will persuade an otherwise resigned soul to rise head above heels one more time to face another day.

HOPE IS EVERYWHERE

Hope is God's gift to all mankind, the imprint of His image that Adam's sin stained but could not erase. The archives of human history are filled with the stories of people who, fueled by foolish hopes and impossible dreams, have overcome tremendous odds to win races, break records, scale unscalable heights, and survive unthinkable conditions. I was privileged to meet one such dreamer and to see the fruit of his hopes in the summer of 1968.

I had just completed my junior year at Oral Roberts University (ORU) in Tulsa, Oklahoma, and now had the opportunity to join Dr. Roberts and a team of fellow students on an overseas tour that began in England, took us across western Europe into Soviet Estonia, and concluded six weeks later in Israel.

As we flew into Tel Aviv in late July, I thought back to what a life-changing trip it had been and what a tumultuous year 1968 was turning out to be. We had landed in London just after dawn on June 6, only to learn that presidential candidate Robert Kennedy had been mortally wounded in California, his death a tragic sequel to the assassination of Dr. Martin Luther King Jr. in Memphis just two months earlier.

London had likewise been the scene of my first date with fellow student Jan D'Arpa, who the following winter became my wife.

The tour had also taken me to the Soviet Union and to

the suffering Christian underground. With one brief prayer meeting, their world had changed mine, and somehow I knew that this first trip there would not be my last.

Now we were in Israel, rumbling across the Negev to the desert home of eighty-one-year-old former Prime Minister David Ben-Gurion, whom *TIME* magazine had characterized as a combination of George Washington and Moses. This was the man who had taught Israel how to fight and, more significantly, how not to fight. To Ben-Gurion, hope was more important than hostility, which was why he had settled here at the kibbutz Sede Boker way back in 1953. "The desert provides us with the best opportunity to begin again," he said. "This is a vital element of our renaissance in Israel. For it is in mastering nature that man learns to control himself." That was why he lived out here. These sands were a blank slate awaiting his pen. They represented hope, and he was Israel's architect of hope.

> *Hope is God's gift to all mankind, the imprint of His image that Adam's sin stained but could not erase.*

As forty-two of us piled off the bus, our renowned host wisely decided to entertain us on the lawn outside his modest, one-story bungalow. A living patriarch, Ben-Gurion was short, stocky, and nearly bald, save for a generous white fringe above his temples. As we sat down on the grass, I looked into his deeply creased face and found myself struck by his sparkling, youthful blue eyes.

Those eyes had plenty of reason to sparkle. A year earlier Israel had won a decisive victory over a vast Arab coalition in the Six-Day War, taking control of much new territory, including Jerusalem and its holy places. Now, pilgrims were coming from around the world by the thousands to pray at the Wailing Wall, and soldiers' stories of angelic assistance during the war were on many lips as well. The whole country was brimming with hope, and Ben-Gurion's grandfatherly pride was easy to comprehend.

But it wasn't recent events that the legendary statesman recalled for us that day. He spoke instead of May 14, 1948, and how he, as the nation's first prime minister and defense minister, had read the fateful proclamation: "We...hereby declare the establishment of a Jewish state in Eretz-Israel, to be known as the State of Israel." He also told us a bit of the history of the Zionist movement and especially about the hopes of a man named Theodor Herzl, the Austrian Jew whom the same Israeli declaration called "the spiritual father of the Jewish State."[3]

Herzl was born in Budapest, Hungary, in 1860, spent his college years in Austria, and eventually became a playwright, novelist, and journalist in Paris. A child of the Enlightenment, he chose the nonreligious life of a modern European secularist and considered his Jewish heritage an anachronism. Jews would get along better, he thought, if they would stop thinking of themselves as a chosen people and get on with the business of being good citizens of Europe.

But in 1895, Herzl's illusions of Euro-Jewish harmony were shattered when a French army captain named Alfred Dreyfuss was convicted of treason. Like Herzl, Dreyfuss had lived as a patriotic Frenchman, not a Jew, and had led an exemplary life in the military. Moreover, the evidence against him clearly had been manufactured and the real facts of his case ignored. It didn't take long for Herzl to realize that Dreyfuss was guilty of only one thing: being a Jew. At that moment he became convinced that "the Jews *were* a special people, always had been a special people, and could be nothing else but a special people. Europeans would hate the Jews whether they lived as an odd people in a ghetto or as modern individuals submerged into Parisian culture. This much Dreyfuss taught him."[4]

On that fateful day, Theodor Herzl realized that there were only two solutions to what Europeans had taken to calling the "Jewish question": statehood or annihilation. Both prospects were frightening, of course, but the former was also oddly exhilarating. Soon Herzl found himself obsessed and then inspired. He began to write feverishly, day and night. "He was not working out the idea. The idea was working him out," said biographer Alex Bein.[5] A glimmer of hope had become a blinding light, and the playwright turned pundit would have to keep writing until his vision cleared again.

> *Hope was alive in the summer of 1968. I saw it in the eyes of an eighty-one-year-old desert dreamer named David Ben-Gurion.*

Write he did, and then, for the rest of his life, Herzl dedicated himself to the singular outlandish hope that constituted the title of his new book: *The Jewish State.* Here is an excerpt from the very end of that work.

> Here it is, fellow Jews! Neither fable nor deception! Every man may test its reality for himself, for every man will carry over with him a portion of the Promised Land—one in his head, another in his arms, another in his acquired possessions.
>
> Now, all this may appear to be an interminably long affair. Even in the most favorable circumstances, many years might elapse before the commencement

of the foundation of the State. In the meantime, Jews in a thousand different places would suffer insults, mortifications, abuse, blows, depredation, and death. No; if we only begin to carry out the plans, Anti-Semitism would stop at once and forever. For it is the conclusion of peace....

We shall live at last as free men on our own soil, and die peacefully in our own homes.

The world will be freed by our liberty, enriched by our wealth, magnified by our greatness.

And whatever we attempt there to accomplish for our own welfare, will react powerfully and beneficially for the good of humanity.[6]

Herzl published his treatise of hope on February 14, 1896, and then worked tirelessly to promote it until he died in 1904, at age forty-four, exhausted and penniless. But his hope did not die with him. Though it would suffer all that he had prophesied, as well as a Hitlerian nightmare, the specter of whose six million Jewish casualties might have killed his vision in its infancy, and though it still has not been fully realized, Herzl's hope did survive.

It lived on, just as he had foretold, in the lives and deaths, sufferings and exploits of other Jews who carried in their hearts and heads their own "portion of the Promised Land." His hope lived beyond his forty-four years for exactly forty-four more, until that sunny day in 1948 when Israel's first prime minister stood to make Israel's declaration of statehood.

Herzl's hope was alive in the summer of 1968 as well. I know, because I saw it, sparkling still, in the bright blue eyes of an eighty-one-year-old desert dreamer named David Ben-Gurion.

THE ANATOMY OF HOPE

Hope must always be tested in order to be proven real, and in the modern world it is tested more often in doctors' offices than perhaps anywhere else. So many dreams have been derailed by diagnoses like *cancer* and words like *inoperable*, so many hopes dashed by suggestions that the future be discussed in terms of comfort rather than a cure. And, of course, if hope dies in the office, there is usually none left for the operating room.

The aforementioned Dr. Jerome Groopman is out to change all that. Rather than seek merely to diagnose his patients, he looks for ways to ignite, or reignite, hope in them.

> When I meet a new patient, listen to his history, perform a physical examination, review his laboratory tests, and study his X-rays, I am doing more than gathering and analyzing clinical data. I am searching for hope. Hope, I have come to believe, is as vital to our lives as the very oxygen that we breathe.[7]

Dr. Groopman knows from personal experience what it is like to live for years without hope and then to experience both the mental and physical rejuvenation that can only happen with hope's permission. After a failed spine surgery in 1979, he spent nearly two decades in what he describes as a "labyrinth of relapsing pain and debility."[8] Scar tissue had formed around the nerves in his lower back, tethering them in such a way that any quick twist or turn, bend or jump, would set him writhing in pain and send him to bed for several days.

After a few such episodes, the young doctor decided to live within what he saw as very narrow limits. For the next nineteen years, "the boundary on my life was like an electrified fence at the perimeter of a prison," he says. "If I ventured too far and tested it, I was thrown back from the shock of its force into my confinement. If I stayed inside the fence, I was somewhat safe."[9] The doctor was so disheartened he even began avoiding doctors.

In the summer of 1999, after a back massage had sent him yet again into crippling spasms, Dr. Groopman found himself at the New England Baptist Hospital, consulting with a physician who specialized in rehabilitation medicine. "I believe you can be freed from your pain," said Dr. James Rainville. "I believe you can rebuild yourself and do much, much more." The specialist saw the skepticism that had long ago chiseled itself into Groopman's countenance.

> "You've lived all these years without any real hope, and it's hard to open that door and glimpse a different kind of life." He paused and then spoke with gravity. "It's your choice: to try or not to try. You can walk out of my office now and believe everything you've believed for the past nineteen years, and live the way you have. Or you can test me. And I'll tell you now, I'm right."[10]

Groopman sat there stunned by the challenge. For a while, he argued with himself about whether or not to admit such an outrageous possibility.

> "How can I test you?" I finally asked.
> "Ignore the pain," Dr. Rainville shot back. "No more worshiping this [volcano god of pain]. No more sacrifices. Just disregard its demands. The pain doesn't mean anything serious. As your mind reorients its beliefs, the pain will lessen."[11]

Those words not only would prove to change Jerome Groopman's life, but they would also change the lives of countless of his patients and readers in years to come. He was already a published author, and the titles of his books from then on tracked the dramatic transformation that took place in his mind and body. *The Measure of Our Days*,[12] a book on suffering, had come out in that nineteenth year of his agony. His next volume, *Second Opinions*,[13] was released in 2001, during his initial year of reconsideration and recovery. By 2004, Dr. Groopman was pain free and living a full and active life. That year his newest release also hit the shelves. It's title: *The Anatomy of Hope*.

> *Hope makes a biological contribution to recovery, with virtually no limit to that contribution. Hope is more a cause of change than a response to it.*

Groopman's recovery had spurred him to explore the subject of hope. But, ever the good scientist, he distrusted his own enthusiasm and chose to let his experience supply him with questions that only rigorous research might answer.

> So I asked, as a scientist, is there a biological mechanism whereby the feeling of hope can contribute to clinical recovery? And if there is such a biology of hope, how far is its reach, and what may be its limits? Or is hope a feeling that occurs along with certain physiological changes but has no causal link to them?[14]

The answers to those three questions turned out to be: yes, hope makes an actual biological contribution to recovery; no, there is virtually no limit to that contribution; and indeed, hope is more a cause of change than a response to it. Among other findings, Groopman discovered that the brains of hopeful people trigger the release of neurochemicals in the body that lessen pain and promote healing.

> It turns out that we have our own natural forms of morphine—within our brains are chemicals akin to opiates. These chemicals are called "endorphins" and "enkephalins." Belief and expectation, cardinal components of hope, can block pain by releasing the brain's endorphins and enkephalins, thereby mimicking the effects of morphine.[15]

The doctor went on to explain that when pain amplifies a sense of hopelessness, the body releases fewer pain-deadening neurochemicals, creating a cycle that continues to increase pain and decrease hope.

> To break that cycle is key. It can be broken by the first spark of hope. Hope sets off a chain reaction. Hope tempers pain, and as we sense less pain, that feeling of hope expands, which further reduces pain. As pain subsides, a significant obstacle to enduring a harsh but necessary therapy is removed.[16]

Jerome Groopman could have opted to stay in his prison of pain all those years ago. He could have decided—like so many scientists and skeptics trained in theories of evolution—to evict hope from the halls of science and consign it to the ghetto of religion. Had he in fact chosen the life of the cold clinician, he would have abandoned not just his own soul but also thousands of others to the labyrinth. Instead, he became the medical establishment's apostle of hope.

We are not prisoners of our DNA. We will likely discover genes that contribute to the very complex feeling we know as hope, but the circuits in the brain that stem from this feeling are not static. Rather, events in our lives modify them, and I would posit that the words spoken and the gestures made by physicians and surgeons and nurses and social workers and psychologists and psychiatrists, and family and friends, influence the [brain's] synaptic connections. No one should underestimate the complexity of factors that coalesce in this biological process. But I interpret it to mean that no one is beyond the capacity to hope.[17]

THE FIRE WITHIN

Hope, in its simplest form, is universal and indispensable, like the sun's light. No one in the world can "see" without at least some small ray of hope to guide them, whether to reach for the stars or merely to retrace yesterday's desperate steps to survive. Without hope we are all blind—lost in the labyrinth.

The late Dr. Viktor Frankl, author of *Man's Search for Meaning*, was often asked why he thought his Holocaust memoir had become a best seller. "I do not at all see in [it] so much an achievement and accomplishment on my part as an expression of the misery of our time," he said. "If hundreds of thousands of people reach out for a book whose very title promises to deal with the question of a meaning to life, it must be a question that burns under their fingernails."[18]

Frankl wrote those words in the preface to his book's 1984 edition in the midst of America's Reagan years. The newly reelected fortieth president of the United States had proclaimed it "morning in America," and in economic terms he was certainly right. The mid-1980s were the dawn of an era of unprecedented prosperity. Yet Frankl's question still burned under a billion fingernails, as it does today, because prosperity does not bring purpose. Money has never equaled meaning.

Finding meaning in life ultimately boils down to answering one even deeper question: *Who lit this fire, and why are we driven to quench it?* In the answer we shall find the hope that underlies all hopes, the wish behind every wish. For centuries, people claiming to know the answer have written books, fomented revolutions, and started religions to make their case, but the short answer is this: *God lit the fire in order to make man search feverishly for meaning that only He can give.*

> And He made from one man every nation of mankind to live on all the face of the earth, having determined their appointed times and the boundaries of their habitation, that they would seek God, if perhaps they might grope for Him and find Him, though He is not far from each one of us; for in Him we live and move and exist, as even some of your own poets have said, "For we also are His children."
>
> —ACTS 17:26–28

Hope is both the fire that makes us search and the lamp by which we search. Like children with a flashlight, we have hope in our hands and want to shine it on something. The desire itself should alert us to the fact that God is waiting to be found, that He wants us to look high and low until at last He is front and center in the beam. Just as hunger in the belly motivates every person on Earth to find food, so the urge to hope that God has sewn into human nature will only be satisfied in finding Him. Educator and author Douglas Wilson describes the innate human hunger for God, comparing it to being "thirsty in a world without water, or hungry in a world without food, or full of sexual desire in a world without another sex, and so on."[19]

Hope, then, shows itself everywhere in life. Its seed is in the child's fantasy that Santa Claus is coming to town, its full flower in the dying thief's sober plea for Jesus to "remember me when You come in Your kingdom."[20] And like all of God's gifts, whether we develop or waste it is up to us. As we shall see in coming chapters, some people's hopes are dashed upon the rocks of repeated disappointment. Others never quit believing in Santa, but they merely shift their misplaced hopes to lotteries or governments or fantasies of fame. Still others stare for so long into clouds of despair that they finally conclude there is no sun.

> *Just as hunger in the belly motivates every person on Earth to find food, so the urge to hope that God has sewn into human nature will only be satisfied in finding Him.*

But some people, like you, keep searching for the one true hope that anchors all others. They are the ones who will not be disappointed but will find themselves in the company of the God of hope, who promises to "fill you with all joy and peace in believing, so that you will abound in hope by the power of the Holy Spirit."[21]

In the meantime, hope drives them to look for more hope. It is, as we said earlier, a gift from the Creator that goes unrecognized by most of its recipients. It is the residue of His image, the echo of *His* hope for them. Hope is God's invitation to come home to Him.

4

STOLEN HOPES

Catch the foxes for us, the little foxes that
are ruining the vineyards, while our vineyards are in blossom.[1]

—KING SOLOMON

THE TINY BALTIC nation of Latvia gained independence
with the collapse of the Soviet Union in 1991. Shortly
thereafter, Betsy Thraves, an American missionary,
went to teach English to young adults at a language school
near the Latvian capital of Riga.

"One day I asked my students to tell me what they wanted to
be in life, what their dreams and goals were. But the normally
talkative class fell silent; nobody would answer me. I asked
them again, thinking they were just being shy. After all, such a
question never would have come up during Soviet times. Life
didn't include many choices back then.

"I persisted, but after a while it became clear they were
stonewalling me. Finally one young man muttered something
under his breath, as he stared down at his desk. 'What did you
say?' I probed. 'Go ahead and say it out loud.'

"'What's the use,' said the sullen student without even making it a question. 'It could never happen anyway.'"

That young man unwittingly spoke for tens of millions of people supposedly "set free" with the collapse of the Eastern Bloc. True, they were no longer under the thumb of the Kremlin, yet the hopelessness that had gripped their parents, grandparents, neighbors, and classmates for more than half a century hung as heavy as chains in their minds too.

"We wake up every morning expecting everything that day to go wrong," one friend said. "That way we're never disappointed. And if anything better than the worst actually happens, it's a nice surprise."

These young people were programmed for hopelessness not because they themselves had witnessed the mass murders of Stalin or had their homes destroyed by war. They had not been personally harassed by the secret police, and in fact, most had entered adulthood during the USSR's increasingly free final days under Mikhail Gorbachev.

> *We have been conditioned like lab rats to live (and die) with low expectations, having hardly any of them in line with the wonderful vision God has cast for our lives.*

Yet they were utterly disillusioned about their futures. Why? Because a thousand "little foxes"—childhood disappointments, parental alcoholism, divorce, economic corruption, and so on—had already eaten away their dreams for success in life at any level.[2]

We brace ourselves for big blows like hurricanes and wars. But King Solomon warned us that the little foxes can destroy our vineyards, that is, the fruit of our lives.[3] The king's metaphor speaks of the kinds of spiritual strongholds that rob us of hope in a thousand little ways as opposed to one gigantic and easily identifiable attack of the devil. More often than not these strongholds are mind-sets rather than outright demonic constructs, but they bring devastation nonetheless.

How many marriages have been destroyed by the little foxes of too much work apart and not enough time together? How many sons have been lost to their fathers by too much time in front of televisions and computers and not enough driveway basketball? How many of us have been *spiritually programmed* by our parents, teachers, and peers never to "get our hopes up" in the first place?

We have been conditioned like lab rats to live (and die) with low expectations, having hardly any of them in line with the wonderful vision God has cast for our lives. "For I know the plans that I have for you," He told His people when they were in captivity, "plans for welfare and not for calamity to give you a future and a hope."[4]

God is still making plans for His people. You might be facing divorce, behind in your bills, battling depression, or in the middle of all three. Perhaps you're fighting cancer, and someone else has told you there's no hope. But the ruler of the universe knows the plan He has for you, and it is a plan for your welfare and not for calamity, to give you a future and a hope.

Six Strongholds

Success author and professional mentor Steven K. Scott, in his book *Simple Steps to Impossible Dreams*, points to six mental strongholds that hold most people back from fulfilling their dreams.[5] I believe he has exposed six of the most insidious of King Solomon's little foxes, six ways in which real hope is aborted before it ever has the chance to grow. Scott lists them, in no particular order, as:

1. Programming for mediocrity[6]
2. Fear of failure[7]
3. Avoidance of criticism[8]
4. Lack of clear vision[9]
5. Lack of know-how[10]
6. Lack of resources[11]

Programming for mediocrity

The world around us has lower expectations for us than God does. This is especially evident in the way we are herded into conformity—and eventual mediocrity—from a young age. Today's educational "experts" often warn parents, with the same ominous tones once reserved for revelations of poor grades, of the dangers of promoting students too quickly. Thus the only way to fit in at school is to not stand out. In a society gone mad with political correctness, too much excellence has become a transgression.

At work, government regulations, corporate policy, and more political correctness have turned gifted men and women into mere numbers, with no incentive to use their full capabilities. We're programmed to be average Joes earning average wages, destined to live in average neighborhoods, where the only way to distinguish one house from another is by a few digits on the mailbox.

Even at church the Christian life often is framed more in terms of avoiding sin than in excelling in righteousness. We learn to become Baptists, Catholics, or Pentecostals, better known to society for leading dull lives than for making the world a better place.

Further ensuring spiritual mediocrity are the false definitions of humility and "modest living" that most Christians accept as God's will. For some reason His desire for us to prosper in all that we do[12] is forgotten, and we embrace the idea that modesty is located just above the poverty line but not *too* far above it.

Complicating the problem is what the late John Wimber called "reverse evangelism," the fact that many Christians live their lives by society's low standards rather than by God's Word. Like the children of Israel a long time ago, we've become fluent in Egyptian when we ought to be teaching Hebrew.

The bottom line is that we've been programmed to live beneath our high calling. So we learn to think of happy, prosperous, world-changing people as someone else, while we cling to the patently unbiblical idea that "this world is not my home." This is why so many Christians meander through life with no sense of purpose on Earth other than waiting to go to heaven. Such aimlessness breeds mediocrity at every turn.

Fear of failure

Steven Scott calls the fear of failure the hardest chain to break, because it "begins to form and take hold in childhood and is usually fully developed and firmly anchored by the time you graduate from high school."[13]

Failure to any degree, especially in childhood, often brings humiliation, and with it an inward promise to oneself that such embarrassment should be avoided in the future at all costs. So instead of learning from failure, most of us vow to avoid it altogether by always playing it safe. We attempt to do only those things we're already sure we can do, thus guaranteeing our "success" at the expense of any further growth.

Of course it isn't success we've ensured, but simply more mediocrity. I could hit home runs over the Pee Wee league fence all day long off the team's best five-year-old pitcher, but that wouldn't make me successful in baseball. Yet the fear of failure keeps millions of Christians in life's minor leagues when God has called them to the majors! Worse than quashing our dreams, the fear of failure prevents us from dreaming in the first place. We'll never measure up to so-and-so's achievements, so why get our hopes up?

Atlanta pastor Andy Stanley, a success by almost anyone's standard, remembers how the fear of failure gained a grip on his life that took years to overcome. The year was 1972, and he was trying out for the eighth grade basketball team.

> Somebody passed the ball to me. I took a shot and missed everything. No rim. No net. No backboard. Nothing. The head coach was standing on the corner of the floor opposite me. He yelled across the court, "Stanley, you've got no backbone." He shook his head in disgust and walked over to the bench.
>
> In a few minutes the scrimmage ended. The tryouts ended. And my chances for playing eighth grade basketball ended as well. But something else happened that night. That coach had cast a vision for me. His words, combined with the events of the evening, painted a picture of my future that took me years to overcome.
>
> I believed him. I believed that in the arena of athletic competition I would never succeed. He told me what I could and should expect in the future in so far as the competitive sports were concerned. He was an adult, a coach, His words cut deep. So I acted on them.
>
> That was the last time I tried out for anything competitive.[14]

Avoidance of criticism

Most people equate criticism with disapproval, which is the exact opposite of what they desire most in life, especially during childhood. If you were to pause right now and examine what you consider to be your main shortcomings, you could probably trace at least some, if not all of them, to criticisms you received in the formative years of your life from individuals whose approval you craved.

> *When your loftiest aspiration has become someone's target practice, it hurts so badly that ending the pain becomes more important than winning the prize.*

"In fact, criticism is so distasteful, disheartening, and painful," says Steven Scott, "that by the time you graduate from grade school, you do everything you can to avoid it. You constantly adjust your behavior, not to achieve what's in your best interest and the best interest of others, but rather simply to avoid being criticized. And the more you care about someone or the higher you regard a person, the more devastating and painful is the impact of their criticism."[15]

This is why so many people abandon their dreams early in life. When their loftiest aspiration has become someone's target practice, it hurts so badly that ending the pain becomes more important than winning the prize. So their dreams wither as they willfully suffocate hope and settle for a life far beneath their "high calling of God in Christ Jesus."[16]

Lack of clear vision

The old saying "If you aim for nothing, you'll hit it" is true. Hope has everything to do with looking ahead and seeing a goal. Yet many people enter adulthood with no more focus than the vague notion that they have to get a job or a degree of some sort. That's OK if their early jobs or studies help them sharpen their focus and sort out more important long-range goals. But a persistent lack of vision can become a lifelong habit.

I'm not a fan of the late Beatle John Lennon, but he made a salient observation years ago when he said, "Life is what happens while you're busy making other plans."[17] So many Christians stumble through life with no sense of destiny, certainly not one they know how to methodically plan for. They had dreams once, way back when they first met Jesus, but then "life happened." One day they awaken to find themselves with careers they never really intended, marriages they entered prayerlessly, and debt that has them in a financial death grip.

For these folks hope never amounts to anything more than wishful thinking, a tinge of regret about what might have been rather than a spark in their hearts that says it's not too late.

Lack of know-how

Lots of people surrender their dreams early in life because they seem too big to fulfill. Millions throw in the towel on marriage because they think they'll never understand the needs of a dissatisfied spouse. Parents give up on troubled teens because they just don't know what to do next.

I grew up a country pastor's kid on the prairies of western Canada. If some grown-up from Dad's congregation had said to me, "Terry, someday you'll stand face-to-face with prime ministers and popes, and you'll even have a hand in the writing of a new constitution for the nation of Iraq," I would have laughed loudly enough to spook the neighbor's cattle. How could a little boy from the prairies ever hope to experience such adventures?

Yet when I was fourteen, a camp-meeting preacher did indeed confront me with a calling greater than I could imagine. He told me that someday I would preach before enormous crowds overseas, painting a portrait of adventure and accomplishment I couldn't begin to envision. At that stage, I didn't know how to get a passport or buy a plane ticket. I didn't know how to work with translators or conduct myself in front of dignitaries. And I certainly didn't know how to preach.

Like so many others before and after me, I could have given up then and there. But unlike so many others, I didn't quit. Instead I "hoped against hope."[18] Even though I lacked the know-how to accomplish this impossible dream, I instinctively realized that I would meet others with the skills I lacked and that God would bring His Word to pass in my life.

Sad to say, most Christians reading these words can remember their own encounter with a dream—it probably came soon after you met Christ—as well as the death of that dream. Perhaps a spouse laughed at your inspiration, like Abraham's elderly wife Sarah laughed at God's words to her husband. Maybe a parent or a teacher, intent on keeping your feet on the ground, smothered it with "common sense." (Albert Einstein became a high school dropout partly on the advice of a teacher.) Or maybe your schoolmates mocked you just enough to cause you to stop studying hard, so you never gained the knowledge you would have needed.

In any case, here you are, your early hopes now hardened regrets.

Lack of resources

The final little fox involves three things we all wish we had more of: time, talent, and money.[19] I've heard so many ministers—especially missionaries—say, "I'd love to accomplish such-and-such, but I just don't have the money."

Over the years I've heard others say, "I'd love to share the gospel with people, but I'm just not good with words." Still others cite the fact that, "With all my duties with my job and family, there's just not enough time left to..." (fill in the blank).

Hope goes unrequited and a destiny unfulfilled because finances stay just a bit too tight, or the learning curve is just a little too steep at your age, or you just don't have enough time.

Maybe it's true that you don't have the resources. But then who or what put that desire in your heart in the first place? And why does the memory of that fire still flicker in your soul? Could it be that a lack of resources—or your *perception* of one—killed a godly hope before it ever got the chance to live?

CATCH THE LITTLE FOXES

So many Christians have let these little foxes slither through the gardens of their lives unnoticed, stealing their fruitfulness, their destinies, before they even had a chance to bud. They've let peer pressure, the criticism of parents or teachers, and the low expectations of society at large rob them of hope.

Millions of Christians live without hope because they have believed the world's lies instead of God's truth. He sees you so differently, so much more optimistically than even the people who love you the most. He says you can be "transformed by the renewing of your mind, so that you may prove what the will of God is."[20] His will for you is far better than any "best" you could ever conceive. The reason that you may have such trouble comprehending it is because you focus on your limitations rather than God's ability to fulfill His Word. But Paul said, "Faithful is He who calls you, and He also will bring it to pass."[21] J. I. Packer says:

Scripture shows God using the oddest, rawest, most lopsided and flawed of his children to further his work, at the same time as he carries on his sanctifying strategy for getting them into better moral and spiritual shape.[22]

A friend of mine tells about his goddaughter, who had disappointed herself so many times that she wondered aloud why he continued expressing great hope about her future. He smiled at her and said, "Sweetheart, I'm simply convinced that God's ability to save your life is greater than your ability to ruin it." I think that's the way that God Himself looks at us. Why else would He choose such nobodies as Joseph, Gideon, David, and Peter, to name just four?

> *So many Christians have let peer pressure,*
> *the criticism of parents or teachers, and the*
> *low expectations of society at large rob them*
> *of hope.*

Joseph was despised by his brothers to the point that they committed crimes against him. He was sold into slavery and could have sunk into despair and died in Egyptian poverty. He was falsely accused and spent twelve years in jail, but Joseph chose to focus upon a dream God had given him as a teenager. He clung to its strange but glorious symbols against all odds of ever seeing it come to pass, working hard in the meantime to show himself approved both to God and man—in his case, Pharaoh. And Joseph made history because he kept hope alive.

Gideon was a terrified youth, hiding in a hole in the ground, when an angel suddenly appeared and greeted him as a "valiant warrior."[23] Gideon rebuffed God's calling at first, citing both social barriers and his own inadequacy, but the Lord persisted in calling him a champion, giving him detailed instructions for winning the war. Even when he finally obeyed, Gideon did so timidly "because he was too afraid of his father's household and the men of the city to do it by day, [so] he did it by night."[24]

Why, then, did Gideon ultimately succeed? How did the young coward become a national champion? Because at a certain point he chose to see himself and his surroundings on God's terms rather than his own. Gideon hoped in God.

What about David? When the prophet Samuel came calling to anoint a king from among Jesse's sons, the sheep farmer left his youngest son, the handsome young musician, out in the field to tend the flocks. David's father didn't recognize the boy's potential to be king; in fact, he used him to run errands between home and the battlefront where his older sons were doing military duty.

> *Make the decision, every morning when you get up, to see yourself that day the way God sees you.*

David's older brother Eliab scolded him, accusing him of insolence for daring to think he could make a difference in the battle. Yet David prevailed, killing Goliath, winning battle after battle, and eventually becoming a king of Israel so beloved that the Scriptures call him "a man after God's own heart."[25]

What was David's secret, especially when his own father didn't believe in him and his brother was against him? *When others saw giants, David saw God.* He won great victories because in his mind they were impossible to lose. David *hoped.*

Then there's Peter. Everyone knew him as Simon, son of John. He was a foul-mouthed fisherman, a social outcast. Yet Simon, at some point, began to see himself the way Jesus saw him. "You are Simon the son of John," said Jesus. "You shall be called Cephas [Peter]."[26] Peter remained impetuous and unreliable for the next three years, yet Jesus never gave up hoping in him, even when the fisherman gave up on himself and ran away in fear for his life. And eventually he became the rock, an architect of Christ's church, because he learned to see himself the way God saw him.

There they are, all six little foxes, working hard against these four men. Joseph faced scathing criticism and a complete lack of resources. Gideon lacked not only resources but also know-how. He freely admitted his fear of failure and exhibited a lack of clear vision as to how to lead an army. David was programmed by his own father and brothers—his peers—for mediocrity, and in the world's eyes he certainly lacked the resources to fight Goliath. Peter was terrified of criticism, even from a young girl.[27] He feared failure as well, sinking beneath the waves even when Jesus stood on the water in front of him.[28] All four of these men, though they had feet of clay, ultimately refused to conform to the world's expectations and decided to see themselves on God's terms. In other words, they hoped in God.

Here is the way to trap the little foxes and kick them right out of your life. Make the decision, every morning when you get up, to see yourself that day the way God sees you. That's precisely why St. James called the Bible a "mirror."[29] You are supposed to see yourself in terms of God's Word. What God says about you must become the rule in your mind. If everyone around you says you're nothing, but God's Word says "greater is He who is in you than he who is in the world,"[30] then *what God says must be your reality.* This is not "mind over matter" but abiding hope—hope that never dims in the least. It is hope that can never be stolen.

5

ILLUSIONS OF HOPE

If we hope for what we are not likely to possess, we act and think in vain, and make life a greater dream and shadow than it really is.[1]

—JOSEPH ADDISON

BILLIONS OF PEOPLE around the world pin their hopes just about everywhere but in heaven. For proof, look no further than the way hope is marketed. The islands of the Philippines offer psychic healers. Chinese markets hawk keychain Buddhas not as trinkets but as idols. And here in America, government-sponsored lotteries are the rule rather than the exception. One would think that such dishonest schemes—they used to be called numbers rackets—would fail since the odds against winning are overwhelming. Yet state governments routinely exploit the wildly unrealistic, misplaced hopes of their poorest citizens, further perpetuating not only their poverty but also the mind-set that keeps them poor.

Money isn't the only place people sink their hopes. In one significant study of 653 middle-schoolers, *fame ranked higher than fortune as their goal in life*.[2] That claim startled me when

I read it, considering that the very famous are—more than anything else—famously miserable. From the premature death of James Dean to the dysfunctional life and death of Michael Jackson, Hollywood has been—and remains—all too happy to provide sound and lights for self-destruction.

> *From the antics of spoiled socialites to the matrimonial merry-go-round of movie stars, hopelessness parades as happiness.*

The late King of Pop, in particular, could serve as the poster child for the misplaced hopes of the rich and famous. Phenomenally successful as an artist and performer (his *Thriller* album is the most successful recording in history with more than 100 million copies sold), Jackson amassed a fortune that by 2007 reached some $236 million in net worth.[3] Sadly, however, the pop icon never managed to overcome the insecurities of his childhood, wasting much of his wealth on a lifestyle that was both lavish and bizarre, as evidenced by his countless plastic surgeries, questionable conduct with children, and lifelong obsession with fantasy. Jackson even patterned his private estate, Neverland Ranch, after the Walt Disney Company's theme parks, complete with zoo animals, adventure rides, and a miniature railroad. But neither makeovers nor make-believe could satisfy Michael Jackson's real-world hunger for happiness. Eventually exhausted emotionally by his quest, the enigmatic star died in 2009, at age fifty, from an illegal sedative overdose.

Today's tabloid-publishing industry is built around scandalizing tragic figures such as Michael Jackson as well as chronicling the vapid lives of people who are famous simply for being famous. From the antics of spoiled socialites to the matrimonial merry-go-round of movie stars, hopelessness parades as happiness in scandal sheets and on cable television. And millions of young minds are drawn to it like moths to a flame.

EUTOPIA

Beyond fame and fortune, many people hang their hopes on a third illusion: political solutions to life's problems. Even though pundits are quick to claim that politics and religion do not mix, reliance on civil government has become a "way of salvation" to millions of people. In other words, politics *is* their religion. Whether talking about poverty, racism, global climate change, education, or a thousand other subjects, they believe there is no ill that cannot be cured either by more government intervention or—for children—"better schools."

Hope in messianic civil government is by no means restricted to America. Since the last pitiful gasps of the Soviet Union in 1991, western European nations, instead of celebrating liberty's triumph, have rushed to embrace their own brand of salvation through centralized government, repudiating their own Christian history in the process. In fact, the 2004 Constitutional Treaty for Europe goes to great lengths to avoid mentioning the foundational role of Christianity in the development of Western civilization, a history that can be traced all the way back to an obscure little rabbi from Tarsus named Saul, who revolutionized European life by preaching another God besides Caesar.

Author George Wiegel has written *The Cube and the Cathedral: Europe, America, and Politics Without God*, in which he quotes the late Pope John Paul II as saying, "The most urgent matter Europe faces, in both East and West, is a growing need for hope, a hope which will enable us to give meaning to life and history and to continue on our way together."[4] The pope then went on to list the "manifestations of this loss of hope."

1. Practical agnosticism and religious indifference

2. Fear of the future

3. Inner emptiness that grips many people

4. A prevailing sense of loneliness

5. Weakening of the very concept of family

6. Selfishness that closes individuals and groups in upon themselves

7. A growing lack of concern for ethics and an obsessive concern for personal interests and privileges, leading to low birth rates[5]

This list is not randomly ordered. The pope saw how Europe's problems began with indifference to the faith, resulting in an emptiness that eventually festered into cynicism and selfishness. His last three observations are particularly tragic. Today's Europeans, for the most part, do not bother to marry since living together outside of marriage makes the inevitable parting less complicated later on. Instead, they prefer what one pundit has described as "lives of perpetual adolescence," where leisure is the holy grail of life's pursuits. Serious obligations are kept to a minimum, and every night is Saturday night. Such an attitude means not only fewer marriages but also fewer births. After all, everyone knows that "having a kid" just ruins one's social life.

A society where the family is vanishing is like a house whose bricks are crumbling: it cannot stand for long. By repudiating Jesus, Europe has embraced a hopelessness that reveals itself in the demographic suicide of plummeting birth rates and fatalism about the future.[6] And I can say from personal experience that the dim, gray look of cynicism and despair that I used to see on people's faces in the Soviet Union is showing itself more and more in the West. Today's Europeans, by denying their Christian heritage, have shut off their only source of true hope: *the risen Jesus.* As St. Paul said, "If in this life only we have hope in Christ, we are of all men the most pitiable."[7]

FEET PLANTED FIRMLY IN MIDAIR

A fourth false hope that has become increasingly popular in the West is religious universalism, also called New Age thinking or postmodernism. You've probably heard a neighbor or classmate say, "It doesn't matter what you believe as long as you're sincere." Or, "We all create our own reality." Or, "You just have to do what's right for you." These are the one-line hymns of universalism, and today they are sung across the USA from sea to shining sea.

> *Europe has embraced a hopelessness that reveals itself in the demographic suicide of plummeting birth rates.*

Universalism in American is traceable to the late 1700s and was a mere speck on our spiritual landscape until it gained a serious foothold during the cultural revolution of the 1960s and 1970s, thanks especially to John Lennon and the Beatles. This philosophy, while related to what has been preached for years in Unitarian and other liberal churches, is really derived from a combination of eastern religions like Buddhism and Hinduism, with a bit of nature worship thrown in.

Buddhism is a form of atheism that ignores the question of God. It's essential teaching is that life is suffering and that the way to extinguish suffering is to extinguish existence. Total extinguishment is called "nirvana." Buddhism's flip side is Hinduism, a form of polytheism that recognizes so many gods—330 million—as to render the very idea of God meaningless. Both religions adhere to the universalist credo that the sincerity of one's belief is more important than its content.

What do these vacuous "faiths" have to say about hope? To a true Buddhist, hope is a meaningless concept, other than the "hope" of eventual nothingness. Hinduism, on the other hand, denies hope through the fatalistic concept of endless reincarnations, with each new life reaping the wages of the previous one. Where the Buddhist is alone in the universe, the Hindu is alone in the crowd, resigned to yet another cycle of hopelessness. And millions of Americans are there to keep them company.

THE IMPOSSIBLE DREAM

The fifth, and perhaps most tragic, example of misplaced hope is found in modern Islam, where young men and women blow themselves to bits as suicide bombers because they have been told that martyrdom—via the killing of infidels—is their only *sure* way of making it to paradise.

If you spend time around Muslims you'll frequently hear the phrase *Insha'Allah*, meaning "if Allah wills it." But don't be misled. When a Christian says, "God willing," there is the assumption of a relationship with that God. But when a Muslim says, "If Allah wills it," there is no relationship and hence no confidence that anything good will happen.

For Christians, Jesus became *Immanuel*, God with us. The transcendent, eternal Son, because of His love for us, humbled Himself to become God with us. To Muslims, however, Allah is a distant, vengeful taskmaster. Christian apologist Ravi Zacharias describes the contrast.

> In Islam, Allah is seen as distant and totally transcendent....But in the Christian faith, there is the nearness of God. We do not go to the Temple anymore to worship; we take the temple with us. This body is the temple of the living God. There is communion; there is intimacy....Osama bin Laden talks about bombs dropping into mosques, attempting to evoke the anger of the radicals. The teaching of Christ is very different from the philosophy of Mr. bin Laden. It is not the building that is sacred; it is the individual who is sacred. In every life he has killed, he has killed a temple of God.[8]

Islam denies that Jesus was raised from the dead, resorting instead either to the "swoon" theory—He almost died but recovered in the cool of the grave—or the "substitute" theory, that the Romans mistook someone else for Jesus and crucified that man. And by denying the true Savior's resurrection, they also deny the possibility of hope.

THE GOSPEL OF SELF-ESTEEM

For our sixth and final illusion of hope, let's come back to the Western world, to the cultural mirrors we call music, movies, and television. All three are showcases for what happens when people hope in themselves instead of God. And why shouldn't they? Today's generation has been fed the *postmodern gospel of self-esteem* from nursery school through graduation. "Believe in yourself." "Do your own thing." Even the U.S. Army appeals to the cult of self with its posters advertising "An Army of One."

In the world of pop music, song after song—including those catchy tunes sung by smiling preteens on Saturday-morning TV—exhorts our young people to do what *they* want to do, to trust *their* feelings, to live life on *their own* terms. Self-love, their headphones blare, is "the greatest love of all," and they have taken it to heart. Fantasies of self-fulfillment have overtaken reality in capturing kids' affections, leaving them with completely unreal expectations in life. What else could motivate hundreds of patently untalented young singers to parade into a Hollywood audition, each one hoping that he or she might make it as America's next pop idol?

No wonder suicide has become an option when fantasies give way to reality, or that homicide happens when fantasies push reality aside. No wonder kids at church these days can quote Spiderman but not Psalm 23. No wonder Santa is more real than Jesus in society's collective mind, not to mention more acceptable.

> *Hope without a real basis amounts to nothing more than fantasy.*

Our culture says it's OK to call yourself a person of faith as long as you don't specify faith in whom, especially if His name is Jesus. You're free to mention God, provided your tone and context assume a small "g" so that it's clear you subscribe to a cosmic force that also goes by whatever name your listener chooses. More and more often these days, public spokesmen are directed to tell the victims of tragedies that their *thoughts* are with them rather than their *prayers*, because the latter might be offensive. As a British friend commented recently, how is simply thinking about victims supposed to help them?

What do godless belief and pointless thoughts say about hope? *Is hope without a basis possible?* The answer is no. Hope without a real basis amounts to nothing more than fantasy.

As we've said before, there is nothing wrong with wishful thinking as long as it is grounded in reality. But fantasy should never be confused with hope.

THE PRETENSE OF HOPE

Author David Augsburger eloquently explains not only what hope is but also what it is not, describing in vivid prose the many false faces that masquerade as hope. We have already exposed some of them, but here are a few more pretenders.

- **Passive patience:**[9] Patience is a godly virtue, but passive patience is actually resignation wearing the mask of hope. This is the Christian who is always "waiting" on God for an answer but really not expecting one.
- **Determined denial:**[10] This is "hope" that ignores reality rather than taking it into account. It is the hope of the gambler who wants to stay at the table for five more minutes because he *knows* his luck is about to turn. It is what one author has characterized as the "agony of deceit."
- **Futurism:**[11] Here is "hope" that longs for tomorrow but doesn't feel much like working today, hope that pines for heaven because it detests the earth. True hope, on the other hand, "is a present confidence, not a fantasy of controlling the future."[12]
- **Learned illusions:**[13] Here is hope that hangs a pretty painting and pretends it's a window on reality. It is the mask of appearances, the illusion that success comes by looking successful. It is also the mask of manipulation, that

certain behaviors will bring love or wealth or control. "If I just keep pretending, just keep believing, just keep clicking my heels together and wishing…"

- **Constant optimism:**[14] Here is the pretender that insists on always looking at the bright side, to the point of ignoring the proverbial "elephant in the living room." In conflict, it presents itself as the spirit of appeasement, the most famous example coming from the 1930s, when British Prime Minister Neville Chamberlain made several large concessions to the demands of Adolf Hitler in the vain hope that the German dictator might stop invading other countries. Chamberlain's actions proved so disastrous that he was forced to resign, leaving his successor, Winston Churchill, to engineer Hitler's defeat.

THE BOUNDARIES OF HOPE

If hope without a basis is pretending, then hope without boundaries is presumption. Boundaries make life livable. Children need them in order to safely explore their freedoms. Societies need them, both for protection and self-maintenance. Hope needs boundaries too, in much the same way that a fire needs a fireplace. Outside the "confines" of a hearth, a fire can easily burn itself out, or worse, burn its surroundings down. Boundless hope is just as dangerous.

A new generation has been taught the exact opposite, of course. Today, educators and advertisers alike encourage children to throw off authority and restraint, teaching them all about their rights and nothing about their responsibilities. The educational establishment in particular has tossed aside such conventions as the rules of grammar, mathematics, and literacy, resulting in a society where young Americans can't read, write, or spell but have great self-esteem and a profound sense of entitlement.

Above all, traditional biblical ethics have been abandoned in favor of either legitimizing sinful behavior as personal "preference" or excusing it as disease. On the one hand, perversion is declared normal, and on the other, bad results are "not your fault." But justifying sin doesn't erase it any more than legalizing murder stops murder.

Moreover, if sin does not exist, then repentance is impossible. And if repentance is impossible, so is hope. (See chapter 9.) The person who shuns self-restraint destroys both hope and freedom. Is the fire free when you take it out of the fireplace? Is a locomotive liberated when someone "frees" it from the confines of those straight and narrow little rails?

> *Educators and advertisers alike encourage children to throw off authority and restraint, teaching them all about their rights and nothing about their responsibilities.*

True hope, as Augsburger points out, flourishes when it accepts its boundaries.

> Our hopes must find their limits before they can achieve their true strength. There is nothing so strong as hope when it knows how to limit itself. In our more childish moments we hope with absolute dimensions. But not everything can be hoped for. Nothing leads to more hopelessness than the naïve dream that anything can be hoped for, that everything desired is within range of hope.[15]

HOW WE GOT HERE

We have looked briefly at six illusions wherein people search for hope: fame, wealth, power, false religion, pretense, and presumption. But what about *our* lives? The average reader of this book, after all, is probably already a Christian believer and a churchgoer. Yet as we noted at the outset, hope is a helmet many Christians leave sitting on the table.[16] Satan then bombards their unprotected minds in one spiritual aerial assault after another, with predictable results: worry, fear, loneliness, self-pity, depression, despair, cynicism, and even thoughts of suicide ravage the Christian community.

One of the saddest facts of our time is that we look and sound so much like the unsaved world around us that there is nothing about us to draw them to Christ. Our addiction to television, our tolerance of "good" music with corrupt lyrics—"Dad, I don't listen to the words"—our willingness to suffer vile company in order to fit in with the crowd, even the family standards we have inherited—all these factors have attacked our spiritual immune systems, dragging us to lower and lower levels of resistance. We have become like Isaiah, who confessed that he was "a man of unclean lips, and I live among a people of unclean lips."[17]

How did this happen?

> *Hope is a helmet many Christians leave sitting on the table.*

To paraphrase the Greek philosopher Aristotle, the human mind abhors a vacuum. If we do not fill it with God's standards, it will be filled soon enough with someone else's. For too long the American church has not offered a comprehensive world and life view, and so we have built our philosophies on the borrowed sands of humanism. The facts that divorce statistics among Christians are as high as the rest of society and that the vast majority of today's Christian young people stop going to church after leaving home for college show how shifting and unreliable those sands have been.

The only answer is to return to the Rock from which we were hewn two thousand years ago and to let His mind be in us.[18] Many Christians seek prayer and counsel because they "need a word from God," yet they don't realize that their desperation for *a word* comes from their deficit of *the Word*. They are scripturally aliterate, meaning that they *can* read the Bible but choose not to. No wonder they're troubled by what may lie ahead. *They ignore their most reliable gauge on the future.*

Every word of God is utterly reliable when obeyed and is "profitable for teaching, for reproof, for correction, for training in righteousness; so that the man of God may be adequate, equipped for every good work."[19] In other words, *all of the Bible is applicable to all of life.* It is the owner's manual for creation and therefore an utterly dependable rock upon which to base your hopes and dreams.

That is exactly what Moses did when, at the age of eighty, he led God's people out of Egypt in direct defiance of Pharaoh. In fact, the Bible's famous "faith" chapter, Hebrews 11, says that he was not afraid of the king and "kept right on going because he kept his eyes on the one who is invisible."[20] The great leader knew that Pharaoh's wealth and power, though highly visible, were mere illusions of the real thing, so he put his trust in the rock-solid, invisible word that God had spoken in his heart.

I encourage you to do precisely the same thing. Forget the illusions foisted upon you by today's false messiahs, from

Michael Jackson to the Maharishi, from Madison Avenue to Capitol Hill. *Learn to speak the language of hope that is called God's Word.* Fill your mind with it. Let it become your vocabulary book, your traveler's dictionary, and your cultural guide. Pray for yourself what St. Paul prayed for the Christians in early Rome, that the "God of hope fill you with all joy and peace in believing, so that you will abound in hope by the power of the Holy Spirit."[21]

> *Many Christians seek prayer and counsel because they "need a word from God," yet they don't realize that their desperation for a word comes from their deficit of the Word.*

Yes, people will notice the change in you. But after they've been around you for a while, they will also notice a change in themselves, in the way they think and talk, for having been with you. They might not understand you as they used to, and they might even disagree with you a bit more often. But the one thing they will know for sure is that the hope you now profess is no illusion. It's the real thing.

WHEN HOPE DIES

Hope is the worst of evils, for it prolongs
the torment of man.[1]
—FRIEDRICH NIETZSCHE

THE LATE DR. Viktor Frankl, founder of a system of psychoanalysis called "logotherapy," was recognized as Europe's leading psychotherapist during the second half of the twentieth century. The Austrian-born Frankl was also a Holocaust survivor who suffered more than three years in Nazi concentration camps, additionally losing his parents, brother, and wife to Hitler's atrocities. He authored twenty-seven books, the most widely read being *Man's Search for Meaning*, his personal account of life in the camps.

Frankl wrote with rare authority about despair and the complete loss of hope. "The prisoner who had lost faith in the future—his future—was doomed," he observed. "With his loss of belief in the future, he also lost his spiritual hold; he let himself decline and became subject to mental and physical decay."[2]

In one stunning story, Frankl described the deadly effects of despair on one of his fellow prisoners, a man he calls "F—,"

who had been assigned to be his block warden. One day F—
confided to Frankl that he had been told in a dream that the
camp would be liberated on March 30, 1945.

> When F— told me about his dream, he was still full
> of hope and convinced that the voice of his dream
> would be right. But as the promised day drew nearer,
> the war news which reached our camp made it appear
> very unlikely that we would be free on the promised
> date. On March twenty-ninth, F— suddenly became
> ill and ran a high temperature. On March thirtieth,
> the day his prophecy had told him that the war and
> suffering would be over for him, he became delirious
> and lost consciousness. On March thirty-first, he
> was dead. To all outward appearances, he had died
> of typhus.... The ultimate cause of my friend's death
> was that the expected liberation did not come and he
> was severely disappointed. This suddenly lowered his
> body's resistance against the latent typhus infection.
> His faith in the future and his will to live had become
> paralyzed and his body fell victim to illness.[3]

More than a weapon in Satan's arsenal, despair is his *goal*.
In fact, other than death, it is perhaps his most earnest desire,
because it is the spiritual counterpart to total paralysis. It
immobilizes its prey, leaving only the eyes and ears working.

"Why go to church?" it whispers. Why undergo the chemo-
therapy? What's the use in talking to your rebellious son or
estranged wife? Why work hard? Why vote? Why give? Why
pray? *Why care?* And when despair is assured of its victim's
undivided attention, it asks the ultimate question: "What's
the point of living?" Frankl dealt with the inevitable subject
of suicide.

The thought of suicide was entertained by nearly everyone, if only for a brief time. It was born of the hopelessness of the situation....I made myself a firm promise, on my first evening in camp, that I would not "run into the wire." This was a phrase used in camp to describe the most popular method of suicide—touching the electrically charged barbed-wire fence.[4]

Running headlong into an electrified fence is probably inconceivable to you. But to many of Viktor Frankl's fellow prisoners, it represented a welcome relief, albeit a false one. People who commit suicide justify it with the idea that dying cannot be as bad as continuing to live in despair. But that is a tragic misconception, based on Satan's vicious lie that there is no hope. Such a distorted perspective is the very nature of despair.

THE NATURE OF DESPAIR

First, *despair is giving up on God.* It is hopelessness, and at its core there is always either a feeling of having failed God or of having been failed by Him. This is as true for atheists as it is for despondent Christians, since atheists know in their heart of hearts that God exists and that they are alienated from Him.[5]

Sometimes despair grips a nation, as it did the Israelites after they heard the pessimistic majority report of the scouts Moses had sent to spy out the Promised Land. "Would that we had died in the land of Egypt!" they cried. "Or would that we had died in this wilderness! Why is the LORD bringing us into this land, to fall by the sword? Our wives and our little ones will become plunder; would it not be better for us to return to Egypt?"[6]

Centuries later, the prophet Elijah would despair of his life, falsely assuming that God's covenant with Israel had failed. "I have been very zealous for the LORD, the God of hosts," he complained. "For the sons of Israel have forsaken Your covenant, torn down Your altars and killed Your prophets with the sword. And I alone am left; and they seek my life, to take it away."[7]

> *At the core of despair there is always either a feeling of having failed God or of having been failed by Him.*

I saw this same defeated spirit in the Soviet Union, whose founder, Vladimir Lenin, had said that a thousand plagues and pestilences were to be preferred above the slightest belief in the existence of God.

Lenin got his wish. At the time of the Soviet Union's collapse in 1991, crime rates were skyrocketing, while life expectancy had plummeted below sixty years. Most people had little or no motivation to work, many assuming that "democracy" was merely a Western recipe for making social welfare work. After seventy years of failed socialism, they were consummate skeptics, adroitly avoiding disappointment by never expecting anything good in the first place. And no wonder, for beneath the rubble of a thousand toppled statues of Lenin lay their hopes, a million times deferred.

Even after the Soviet collapse, many Christians assumed it was simply too late for Russia and the other former republics to be saved. But they were—and are—wrong. The fact that God brought down the Soviet system after seventy years should spur great hope in every heart that He can finish what

He started in 1991 and bring these hurting people into the kingdom of His love.

Likewise, Israel was mistaken when they accused God of sending them to the slaughter. Even though it took them forty years, they went on to conquer the Promised Land. Elijah needlessly despaired as well. In reality, the number of Jews remaining faithful to God had dwindled to a mere seven thousand, yet God held out that statistic as a sign of *hope* to the beleaguered prophet.[8] Even though the nation had largely given up on Him, the Lord of history had not given up on them.

There is a pattern here that reveals a second aspect of despair: *despair believes that lies are true.* For example, Charles Darwin postulated that man evolved from inanimate matter in a sort of cosmic accident. If we accept Darwin's theory, then we also have to conclude that man has no purpose for his existence, that life is meaningless, and that morality is nothing but a useful tool for our continued survival as a species. Such a view is distorted and unreal, yet scientists, educators, and politicians around the world have embraced it, rejecting the existence of God in the process. The tragic result of accepting Darwin's false reality has been a harvest of death and destruction, the scope of which is unsurpassed in human history. From the killing fields of Cambodia to Josef Stalin's wholesale slaughter of his fellow Russians, the belief that man is merely a highly evolved animal has only caused men to act like animals. If suicide is one extreme on the measure of despair, genocide is the other.

HOPE DIES, HOPE LIVES

Tuesday, November 27, 2007, was a frigid, windswept day in Tulsa, Oklahoma, and the blowing cold stung my face as I hurried across the campus of Oral Roberts University. I was eager to get through the doors of the Learning Resources Center, not only to escape the weather but also to avoid the swarm of reporters and television cameras that had gathered outside. It was D-day for the school. Without an infusion of several *million* dollars in the next five hours, ORU would be forced to close its doors. One of America's most famous Christian universities was on the brink of shutting down, and the world was watching.

Despair believes that lies are true.

I entered the elevator and watched the numbers rise to six, then stepped out onto the private floor that housed not only the school's senior administration but also the Regents Room, an eight-tiered theater where the forty-one-member Board of Regents gathered twice a year to conduct the university's most important business. These hallows had been off limits to me as a transfer student in 1968, but now, after twenty-three years as a regent, I could have walked them blindfolded. Appointed to the board in 1984, I had served my alma mater with deep affection. The school was in my DNA. My missions ministry had started at ORU; five of my six children had attended there; and the university's founder, the late Oral Roberts, had been a close friend. But these strong ties had lately become even stronger with my engagement to English professor Barbara Wolfer, who, along with the rest of the faculty, had gathered in a lecture hall on a lower floor to await—and pray for—the outcome of our meeting. Without a miracle, she and nearly a thousand other wonderful employees would be jobless by nightfall, and the thousands of students we all loved so much would have to go home.

I walked into the Regents Room and down the steps to the handsome, light brown leather chair and curved table that awaited me on the first row. The small brass plaque on the table's suede surface had borne my name for more than two decades. This was *my* place at ORU; it represented a position of responsibility that I had always viewed as an honor but more recently with growing unease.

False accusations against ORU President Richard Roberts and his wife, Lindsay, had lately filled the nation's airwaves as scandal-hungry newspapers and television networks did their best—*worst*—to feed the skepticism of a public long wary of TV preachers. Virtually every charge against the Robertses had been disproven, but vindication usually makes the back page; by now the damage had been done. Richard's nation-wide television program, which had succeeded his father's broadcasts as the school's primary source of funding, was flagging badly. The resultant decline in income had been so overwhelming and so precipitous that as the Board of Regents we faced the need to take immediate, drastic action. But we had already searched every file, combed over every balance sheet, rifled every drawer, and prayed every prayer. The school was dead broke. If we didn't obtain eight million dollars by 5:00 p.m., Oral Roberts University's forty-four-year history would come to an end.

After the requisite formalities, Chairman George Pearsons gave an official summary of our predicament and opened the floor for discussion. But the mood was somber. What could we do? What was there left to say?

Discussion had barely begun when Billy Joe Daugherty, the board's treasurer, asked permission to introduce two guests, Oklahoma City businessmen David Green and his son Mart, principal owners of several successful businesses, including Mardel, a chain of Christian bookstores, and Hobby Lobby, whose 432 "home creativity centers" operate in thirty-four states. They had requested to see the board, explained Daugherty, because Mart had an important petition to present.

Green took the floor and began talking. He had recently secluded himself for forty days of prayer and fasting, he said, and although at the start he had felt nothing more than an urge to pray and seek God's presence, he had found himself increasingly moved to pray for ORU. Only one day after his fast had concluded, he added, did he learn that President Richard Roberts had just resigned. By that time he believed God had spoken to him to loan the university eight million dollars, ask the Board of Regents to replace themselves, and to take over the school's governance. "ORU has a future," he said, smiling, as he held up the check.

It's impossible to describe the elation that swept over all of us at the sight of a man standing there, holding eight million dollars in the air. Rejoicing, laughter, "praise the Lords," and long sighs of relief filled the room. *Hope* filled the room. We were going to make it after all! ORU had a future—we could see it! We could see thousands of future graduates continuing to take salvation, healing, and badly needed expertise around the world, to those places "where God's voice is heard small and His light is dim," as Oral Roberts himself had said all those years ago. The moment was electric.

But it was also just that: a moment.

The hubbub had subsided only slightly when our financial advisor, banker J. D. McKean, spoke up. "We can't receive this money," he said, eliciting a collective gasp that brought the room to silence. "The university has other loans outstanding, and some of them contain clauses that prohibit our borrowing from anyone else until they have been repaid," he explained. "It's an untenable situation. We can't take the money."

That was when hope died. Then and there, before it had a chance to breathe, it died. I can still remember the heaviness. All around the room shoulders dropped and heads lowered. People sank back down into their chairs; one or two leaned forward, faces in their hands. What in the world were we going to do now?

Mart Green and his father took their leave, and the board began debating other proposals. There had been talk of linking ORU with Pat Robertson, founder of Regent University in Virginia Beach. Had there been any word from him? What about the financial plan that had been proposed by the bank in Oklahoma City? An hour passed, and now it was four o'clock. We *had* to have eight million dollars in the bank within the next sixty minutes. The end was near.

> *That was when hope died. Then and there, before it had a chance to breathe, it died.*

Just then the Greens walked back into the room. Mart's eyes were wet, and he shook a little as he held up the check once more. The Lord had spoken to him quite clearly, he said. The money was to be a gift, with no strings attached. That meant, of course, that we could take it and refuse to give him governance, although he still believed that God wanted him to take the reins of the university and put it on a solid foundation for the future.

Jubilation erupted once again as everyone leapt to their feet and began to shout for joy. The hopelessness that had gnawed at our spirits all day was gone for good. Treasurer Daugherty embraced the Greens, thanked them, and handed the check to a courier who made a mad dash for the elevator and a car waiting outside. The money had to be deposited within mere minutes or all the shouting would be in vain.

As the courier left for the bank, the rest of us descended to the floor where most of the faculty and administration members were still waiting. As we entered the back door and walked through the waiting crowd, I looked around the room at one familiar face after another. I had been around ORU for forty years, and some of these people were already teaching when I arrived. Everything was on the line for them—not just their jobs, but four decades of their lives.

I glanced at Barbara and could see the apprehension in her eyes. She loved this place, loved her profession and her students. Her passion for God and His people was one of the qualities that had drawn me to her in the first place. I could see that the tension was almost unbearable for her. I gave her a slight wink to relieve the pressure and quickly looked away as George Pearsons approached the microphone. He wasted no time. God had just given ORU an eight-million-dollar gift from the Green family, he announced, and two million dollars more had been added by J. D. McKean, the banker from Oklahoma City.

The room exploded with joy! From gray-haired professors to twenty-something secretaries, people all over the auditorium hugged one another, crying and laughing and shouting as if they had won a war. And they had! They had fought against disappointment, disenchantment, and despair, and *they had won*. Like Abraham, who was ready to sacrifice his son Isaac on the altar because "he considered that God is able to raise people even from the dead,"[9] they had put ORU on the altar before God. They had trusted God "in hope against hope."[10]

Today, the power of hope is transforming Oral Roberts

University. Thousands of alumni have gotten on board to support the school, and the debt that once stood at $55 million has been, on the very day of this writing, finally retired. The university campus is undergoing an impressive renovation that is exceeded only by the one taking place in the hearts and minds of the thousands of students, faculty, and supporters whose renewed vision is propelling the school into a glorious future. Hope is alive and well at Oral Roberts University.

Stepping Into Your Future

When you first gave your life to God, you might have been in credit card debt up to your neck or in the middle of a messy, irretrievably broken relationship, yet somehow you still felt as free as a bird. Somehow you *knew* everything would work out, because you had learned that "with God all things are possible."[11]

What changed? Have you become more "realistic" about life since then? Are you older and wiser now, or have you spent more time watching the evening news than reading the Good News? "Oh, but the world is in such bad shape," you say. Yes, there seems to be trouble all around, that's true. But God has promised that when spiritual darkness becomes pervasive, "the Lord will rise upon you and His glory will appear upon you. Nations will come to your light, and kings to the brightness of your rising."[12]

Almighty God allows the darkness of the world to get thoroughly, utterly dark for one reason and one reason alone: to draw the world's gaze to the unmistakable light of His people as we "arise and shine" to reflect the glory of the One who shines on us. Nations will come to our light. Think of that! There should be something about us that the people of the world find irresistible, something that even attracts the attention of government leaders in those nations where darkness historically has ruled. This is why Jesus Himself exhorted us, "Let your light shine before men in such a way that they may see your good works, and glorify your Father who is in heaven."[13]

You *can* throw off the blinders of despair and see the world again through the eyes of hope. God has given you this power through the "living hope through the resurrection of Jesus Christ from the dead."[14]

The bottom line is this: If Jesus is not risen from the dead, there is no hope for anyone in the world. If He is risen from the dead, there is no one in the world beyond hope. *There is hope for you!*

THE VOICE OF HOPE

Jesus looked at him and said, "You are Simon the son of John; you shall be called Cephas" (which is translated Peter [the rock]).[1]

—JESUS

YOU MIGHT THINK the Bible is a book about heroes and holy men, superspiritual people who never failed and always did the right thing. But the truth is, it features an all-too-human cast of failures who were transformed by the grace of God to accomplish great good. Think there's no hope for you? Just take a quick look at the people who changed their world: Moses, King David, and the apostle Paul were all murderers, yet among them they wrote at least nineteen of the Bible's sixty-six books. Moses's brother, Aaron, Israel's first high priest, led the nation into idolatry. Samson, the strongest man in the world, had a fatal sexual addiction. Jonah, the prophet God sent to evangelize the people of Nineveh, was so prejudiced against his audience that he was disappointed when God forgave them instead of killing them. The apostle

Matthew was a tax collector, strong-arming his fellow Jews on behalf of the Roman government.

Adam and Eve had started the snowball rolling way back in Eden when they rebelled against God. Then, only a few years later, their firstborn, Cain, killed his younger brother Abel in cold blood. From that time on, sin and evil spread across the world like a blight, until within a few hundred years "the LORD saw that the wickedness of man was great on the earth, and that every intent of the thoughts of his heart was only evil continually."[2] At that point the Creator would have destroyed all earthly life, had it not been for the presence of one promising man, Noah, and his family.

> *You may have been a "doubting Thomas" all your life, convinced you'll never change, but your failures qualify you for greater transformation.*

Even the genealogical tree of Jesus Himself, while composed of many faithful men and women, is a bit of a rogue's gallery: First there was Abraham, the so-called "father of the faith," whose initial disbelief resulted in two sons, Ishmael and Isaac, who hated one another so fervently that their descendants, the Arabs and Jews, have vehemently fought one another ever since. Two generations after Abraham came Jacob, a scheming mama's boy wily enough to trick his older brother out of his inheritance. Then ten of Jacob's sons conspired to sell their own sibling Joseph into Egyptian slavery. The list continues: there was Perez, the product of Judah's incest; Rahab, a prostitute; David, a murderer *and* adulterer; Solomon, who for political reasons foolishly took a thousand wives and concubines—you get the picture. The path that led to the peace and serenity of

Bethlehem's nativity scene featured more than a few detours through history's seamier neighborhoods.

But what happened when the Bible's league of rejects encountered God's grace? Abraham believed God and became the father of all who believe. Moses led God's people to a land of promise. Jonah preached and a nation turned to God. David repented and served the Lord so faithfully that God Himself called him "a man after My own heart."[3] Rahab the harlot risked her life to save God's servants and subsequently made history not as a harlot but as a heroine.

In the New Testament a murderous rabbi named Saul met Jesus in a vision and then became Paul, the most prolific missionary in history as well as the writer of thirteen books of the Bible. And "doubting" Thomas, the disciple who was last to believe in Jesus's resurrection, was so transformed that he dedicated his life to spreading the gospel eastward, starting the first churches in Iraq and then in India.

The message should be clear: God turns abject failures into spiritual champions and then uses them to change the world! That is why I have hope for you and me. You also may have failed in some pretty spectacular ways—I know I have. Perhaps you betrayed a vow or pursued illicit relationships like Samson. You might have exploited people like Matthew or abused your authority like David. You may simply have been a "doubting Thomas" all your life and are convinced you'll never change, *but your failures only qualify you for greater transformation.*

Please note the lack of an exclamation point on that last statement. I am not cheerleading, nor am I expressing faith in your innate ability to change yourself. For all I know, you have picked up this book as a last resort before completely throwing in the towel. I simply know firsthand the transforming grace of God to take a rebellious, drunken Canadian teenager and turn him into a vessel He could use to touch thousands of lives, from the flood-ravaged villages of Indonesia to the bloody streets of Baghdad. And I know that if God could change me, He can change anyone. *I have greater confidence in God's ability to transform you than in your ability to fail.*

HOPE REBORN

We usually think of despair as an individual problem, a jail with one prisoner, but hopelessness can afflict a nation as well. Such was the case when I first visited Iraq in early 2003 before the war of liberation against Saddam Hussein. Everywhere I went, reaction to the notorious strongman's name was the same: a reprimanding *ssshhhhh*, a flash of panic in the eyes, and hastily closed doors, windows, and drapes. Tension and fear would fill the room as panicked hosts stopped in their tracks and waited for the sound of jackboots on the pavement outside. Neighbors often reported neighbors in Saddam's Iraq, and the dictator's thugs were all too happy to try, convict, and execute suspected enemies on the spot. From Mosul to Basra, the word *hope* might as well have not existed.

But when Saddam and his monstrously evil sons Uday and Qusay were executed, the chokehold was broken, and the nation could breathe again. "Terry, we now have four times as many young people getting married as before the war," Dr. Mowaffak al Rubaie, the new naional security advisor, told me excitedly. "Since the liberation, the people of Iraq feel that they have a future. Hope has arisen in our nation." I believe him, and the latest figures in birth rates—which are now nearly twice those of neighboring Iran—tell me that Dr. al Rubaie is still rejoicing today.[4]

Ironically, the West now faces its own crisis of hope. As I write, our federal government is bailing out banks to cover bad mortgages, nationalizing major automobile companies, and attempting to take over health care. From soccer moms to Congress, we have spent our way into financial ruin, and now our leaders think we can spend our way out of it. They calmly speak in terms of *trillions* of dollars as though anyone—including they themselves—is capable of comprehending such staggering numbers. And where does this wealth come from? These same leaders just print more money and then pretend it's real. America has fallen for the old Russian joke about two peasant women who made a good living doing each other's laundry.

Millions of hardworking people have seen their hopes disappear along with their jobs, foreclosed homes, and withered retirement accounts. Yet, ironically, many of them are putting even *more* stock in political solutions, even though the nation's problems are fundamentally spiritual. They will be disappointed, of course, because no civil government ever made a good god.

Yet America is by no means beyond hope because there are also millions who have refused to cast their lot with socialism or bow the knee to the idols of greed and envy. Instead they continue to hope in God. One of them is Robb Baldwin, whose Florida-based investment company, Trade PMR, experienced rapid expansion during the nation's economic downturn. Jim Gilbert asked Robb to explain his success in the midst of failure. Had he simply managed to read the financial tea leaves more accurately than his peers?

"Not at all," he replied emphatically. "A few years ago I had experienced some moderate success but also a lot of failure. In fact, I had made some pretty big mistakes in life, both economically and in other areas, and I came to a point of reckoning: either God's Word was true or it wasn't. So I began looking at the Scriptures from an economic standpoint and decided to let God's Word rule my personal life and professional strategy from then on. Even today, while I'm driving to work, I say aloud what the Bible says about me, about my business, and about the God I serve. When the economic crisis hit in 2008, I knew what I did and did not have to do. And one thing I didn't have to do was to participate in the recession. I'm far from worried. To the contrary, I have great hope for the future."

VOICES OF HOPE

America needs to hear from people like Robb Baldwin, voices of hope in the midst of fear. Our nation has historically been a beacon of hope to the rest of the world. That is why so many desperate people have risked life and limb climbing, tunneling, and treading water to get here. To them, the letters U-S-A spell hope. This is the place where they can stand up and say, for the first time in their lives, "I can." "I can stand on my own." "I can provide for my children." "I can build a life worth living here."

Hope is indispensable for generating enthusiasm, creativity, enlightened decision making, and effective action. More than oil, ethanol, hydrogen, and nuclear power—hope is a nation's most important, most precious source of energy. But hope cannot be managed by bureaucrats or decreed by presidents. Only the God of hope can give hope, yet He will not force it. You and I must choose to receive hope from Him and then put it to work in an increasingly hopeless world.

The Roman Christians of the first century suffered constant persecution from the Caesars, especially Nero. Like most oppressed peoples, they had to survive day by day. Embracing a paradigm of hope would mean looking forward and keeping their heads up; under the weight of their burden that would be difficult. That is why St. Paul closed his letter to the Romans by emphasizing hope to a degree they had never heard before, assuring them that the God of hope would cause them to "abound in hope."[5] The idea of abounding means to overflow with something, to have enough for yourself and others around you. It had to have been nothing short of revolutionary to believers accustomed to meeting in secret, whose natural tendency would have been to keep their faith in Jesus to themselves.

> *Hope is indispensable for generating enthusiasm, creativity, enlightened decision making, and effective action.*

My first encounter with persecuted Christians came in 1968, when I went to Tallinn, Estonia, in the Soviet Union with a student group from Oral Roberts University. There I met several young Estonians who had been expelled from college for nothing more than professing Christ. Others had been—or would be—arrested for leading their friends to Him. At least one, a Methodist youth leader, would later spend two years in prison for his church work. Yet they all served God with a depth of joy that I had never seen before and were dedicated to sharing their faith in Jesus, regardless of the obvious cost.

For the next ten years, the memory of those young faces stirred within me a growing hope to return, and in 1978 I took Living Sound, my team of "musicianaries," back to Tallinn. Now it was our turn to stir their hopes, and we did so with all our hearts. Within two years, even the Associated Press was reporting on the Christian faith of Estonia's young people.

Hope spurs action and ignites faith. It lit a fire in me to return to the USSR and motivated my Estonian friends to persevere during hard times. That is why St. Paul described hope as our incentive for change rather than our longing for heaven. The apostle's life was an example of transforming hope. He had already taken the gospel of Christ across the Mediterranean world from Jerusalem to the Adriatic Coast and was now planning on stopping in Rome on his way to Spain. Having preached in Israel, he was a tireless pioneer in raising up community after community of Gentile believers all over the known world. Only one force could have given a man that kind of strength and motivation: hope—not just the hope of his personal resurrection and eternity with Christ, but hope for the world, then and there. "One thing I do," he said. "Forgetting what lies behind and reaching forward to what lies ahead, I press on toward the goal for the prize of the upward call of God in Christ Jesus."[6]

Paul's encouragement and personal example gave the church in Rome such hope that they not only persevered but also prevailed. Eventually the empire fell into their hands. Do we not have the right to harbor similar hope for the world today? And if so, why should we keep silent about it? The world needs hope. Now.

THE VOICE OF HOPE

Everyone longs for hope, and in most cases it is either fanned into flame or extinguished with words. King Solomon had it right: "Death and life are in the power of the tongue."[7]

Jesus constantly spoke life-giving words of hope to those around Him. Look, for example, at Zaccheus, the famously short tax collector who climbed a tree to see the Savior over the people's heads. He was a notorious swindler and a cheat, yet Jesus shocked the crowd and spoke hope over this outcast by proclaiming, "Today salvation has come to this house, because he, too, is a son of Abraham."[8]

The Lord often turned the tables on public opinion. John chapter 8 tells of a woman caught in the very act of adultery whom the scribes and Pharisees brought to Jesus for trial. The Savior, however, tried the accusing mob according to their own distorted application of the law.[9] Then, after the last embarrassed witness had walked away, He asked the astonished but relieved adulteress if anyone was present to condemn her. "No one, Lord," she said. Then came stunning words of hope: "I do not condemn you, either. Go. From now on sin no more."[10] And with that a woman as good as dead was freed—more than that, *free*.

Even in the midst of excruciating pain and torture, Jesus spoke words of hope to a criminal dying on the cross next to His own. "Jesus, remember me when You come in Your kingdom," the condemned man cried. The Savior, Himself nearing death, saw that faith had arisen in his fellow prisoner's midnight hour and responded with compassion. "Truly I say to you, today you shall be with me in Paradise."[11] What hope to give to a dying man!

It was in choosing His first disciples, however, that the Lord demonstrated most vividly the power of spoken hope. In a society religiously dominated by the conceits of the Pharisees, scribes, and Sadducees, Jesus chose fishermen, tax collectors, publicans, and sinners, "unlearned and ignorant" in the words of Luke.[12] "This crowd which does not know the Law is accursed," the elites had said of the throngs following Jesus,[13] and these crusty Galileans ranked far below the masses. Yet, incredibly, these men were, in author Robert Coleman's words, "the vanguard of [Jesus's] enveloping movement."

> "Through their word," he expected others to believe
> in him (John 17:20), and these in turn to pass the
> word along to others, until in time the world might

know who he was and what he came to do (John 17:21, 23). His whole evangelistic strategy—indeed, the fulfillment of this very purpose in coming into the world, dying on the cross, and rising from the grave—depended on the faithfulness of his chosen disciples to this task. It did not matter how small the group was to start with so long as they reproduced and taught their disciples to reproduce. This was the way his church was to win—through the dedicated lives of those who knew the Savior so well that his Spirit and method constrained them to tell others. As simple as it may seem, this was the way the gospel would conquer. He had no other plan.[14]

This was a radical hope on Jesus's part. The Savior had just three years to select and groom His successors. He could not afford to make mistakes, yet He chose this motley dozen, and even this carefully vetted group included a betrayer. A closer look at one of the Twelve reveals the heart of Jesus's amazing plan.

THE LOOK

St. Peter wasn't always the eloquent preacher of Pentecost and an apostle of Jesus Christ. No, he was just Simon the son of John—Simon Johnson—an uncouth, unreliable, sometimes cowardly fisherman even *after* Jesus had worked with him for three years. Moreover, his brother Andrew had been quicker to show an interest in spiritual matters, initially introducing Simon to Jesus. The Bible says that "Jesus looked at him and said, 'You are Simon the son of John; you shall be called Cephas' (which is translated Peter)."[15]

Jesus looked at Simon Peter the way the sculptor Michelangelo looked at slabs of marble. Once, when asked about the technique he had employed in shaping a particularly beautiful statue, the father of the Renaissance replied, "I saw the angel in the marble and carved until I set him free." So it was with Peter. The Lord saw not only the man who was but also the man who would be. It was quite a stretch.

Our English Bible says Jesus *looked* at Simon, but the verb that John used actually means that He peered at him with "clear discernment." In other words, the Lord cast a penetrating gaze at Simon; He looked *into* him. He could see the roots of the man's character. Nothing was hidden from Him. Peter was rash, hot-tempered, irrational, unstable, and weak-natured. That must have been obvious to everyone on the lake. Jesus could see it all too, yet He hoped in spite of what He saw. He looked at this raw slab of humanity not with the blind optimism of a Pollyanna but with the insight of a Michelangelo, so that the reality of Simon's present was overruled by the Master's vision of his future. The coming transformation would be so complete that Jesus immediately gave him a new name. "You are Simon the son of John; you shall be called . . . Peter."

Jesus needed steady, reliable men like Andrew, not weak, unstable people like this one. Yet by speaking words of hope, He reshaped Simon's heart and attitude about himself. He created a new destiny for "Simon the son of John" at the very moment He changed his name.

The fisherman must have been amazed. *He knows everything about me, but still He calls me a rock!* His heart exploded in hope. Who he was no longer mattered; now he knew *who he would be.*

Yet Peter's greatest failure still lay ahead of him. It came three years later, when Jesus had gathered His disciples to celebrate Israel's annual feast, commonly called the Passover. Rather than celebrating, however, the Lord began talking about His imminent betrayal and death as He washed the disciples' feet. Then He turned and spoke to Peter, curiously reverting to his previous name.

> "Simon, Simon, Satan has asked to sift each of you like wheat. But I have pleaded in prayer for you, Simon, that your faith should not fail. So when you have repented and turned to me again, strengthen your brothers."
>
> Peter said, "Lord, I am ready to go to prison with you, and even to die with you."
>
> But Jesus said, "Peter, let me tell you something. Before the rooster crows tomorrow morning, you will deny three times that you even know me."[16]

The events of the next twenty-four hours played out exactly as the Lord predicted, with Peter's first two denials of Jesus coming within minutes of His arraignment before the high priest. But people weren't buying it. They were still pegging him as an associate of the condemned. An hour later, when he had been recognized for a third time, the panicked disciple "began to curse and swear, 'I do not know the man!'"[17] Again, don't let the English fool you. Peter's "curse" was a strong Aramaic word, tantamount to saying, "May God strike me dead if I'm lying."

> *Hope is the way God sees you, even if, right now, like Peter, you're in the middle of the biggest failure of your life.*

Only Luke records what happened next. "Immediately, while he was still speaking, a rooster crowed. The Lord turned and looked at Peter."[18] That was all it took. One look from Jesus and Peter was cut to the heart. I've often thought about what was in "the look." I believe it was exactly the same penetrating gaze He had given Peter on the day they met, the look of hope that said, "You are, but you shall be."

St. John's Revelation of Jesus Christ describes the Lord's eyes as "a flame of fire."[19] If you're like me, you've probably always thought of that phrase in terms of God's judgment, since fire is known to melt or consume whatever it touches. But Peter's story shows that it was grace, not displeasure, that looked right through him that night.

God's grace is indeed a fire, not overlooking sin, but burning through it to see the good work He has started and still intends to complete. It is the look of hope, and it is the way God sees you, even if, right now, like Peter, you're in the middle of the biggest failure of your life.

YOU ARE—YOU SHALL BE

Names carry a lot of spiritual and psychological weight. We attach connotations to them based on the persons—friend, foe, or famous—who bear them. For example, not many people christen their sons "Judas" or "Adolf," while "Mary" is one of history's most popular names.

Renaming Peter was far more effective than if Jesus had simply called him a rock. It meant that everyone else *also* had to call him a rock. Even more important, it meant that Peter had to call himself a rock.

It might be an encouragement to hear your dad call you a champion, but what if your parents actually gave you a name like that? Such was the case with the Fails in Oklahoma, whose son grew up to become a very successful real estate developer. From his infancy, the boy heard his parents, friends, school mates, and eventually his admirers constantly call him what his wise, clever parents had named him: Never Fail.

It is paramount that you call yourself what God calls you rather than argue with Him about it. Yet so many people, Christians included, adopt *de facto* names that are far beneath heaven's point of view. They say, "I'm so stupid," even though the Bible says, "We have the mind of Christ" (1 Corinthians 2:16). They call themselves weaklings and failures, although God calls them "more than conquerors" (Romans 8:37, NKJV). They resign themselves to decades of depression based on a family name and the baggage that came with it. How many curses have been passed from one generation to the next with words like, "It's no use. I'm just like my old man"?

If you're going to call yourself names, why not call yourself the names God calls you?

- You say you'll never break free from guilt, but God says you are free forever from condemnation.[20]
- You say you don't deserve another chance, but God says the blood of Jesus is continually cleansing you from all sin.[21]
- You say nothing ever works out for you, but God says all things work together for your good.[22]
- You say you're fed up with hypocrites in the church, but God says you're a member of Christ's body.[23]
- You say you'll never make it without your husband, but God says you are more than a conqueror through Christ who loves you.[24]

- You say you're ugly. Who'd want to marry you? But God says you are created in His image after His likeness.[25]
- You say you're the wrong color. You'll never fit in. But God says you are accepted in the Beloved.[26]
- You say you're never going to get well, but God says by His stripes you are healed.[27]
- You say you don't know how you're going to raise your kids as a single mom, but God says you can receive mercy and find grace to help in time of need.[28]
- You say your neighborhood is going to the dogs, but God says you are the salt and light of the world.[29]
- You say your professor makes a fool of you for believing, but God says men will see your good works and glorify Him.[30]
- You say you'll never get that promotion, but God says He is confident that the good work He started in you will be perfected.[31]
- You say the world is going to hell, and you can't make a difference, but God says to go in your strength and save your nation.[32]
- You say your life is going nowhere, but God says He has appointed good works for you to walk in.[33]
- You say you feel so alone in the world, but God says nothing can separate you from His love.[34]

Vision Casting

Jesus constantly spoke hope to people, which is probably why He was so welcome in the homes of religious outcasts, and undoubtedly why both the gospels of Mark and Luke say that "parents brought their children to Jesus so he could touch them and bless them."[35] Just imagine what the God of love would have to say to a little child perched on His knee.

"Johnny, I know you're confused about why your daddy went away so suddenly, and I know it must be really hard on your mother and you to make it by yourselves. But God is going to take care of you, and you're going to grow up to be a very good carpenter."

"Mary, I can tell you have a heart that is drawn to praise God and a beautiful voice to go with it. You keep practicing and singing, because one day you'll bless many people with your music."

> *It is paramount that you call yourself what God calls you rather than argue with Him about it.*

Your words of hope have the power to set other people free. *You cast visions of hope or hopelessness for yourself and others by your words every day.* When you speak to your children, spouse, friends, and work mates, your mouth is the key to awakening—or dashing—hope in them.

The late Oral Roberts, one of the twentieth century's most persuasive evangelists, stuttered badly as a child. As the youngest of five preacher's children, he was reared in the church, but by his teens he had grown to dislike it intensely. "I had had enough of religion. It held no interest for me," he later recalled, even though his mother, Claudia, had promised God, before Oral was born, that her son would "preach the gospel, pray for the sick, and do other impossible things for God."[36]

In 1935, the teenager collapsed during a high school basketball game and was subsequently diagnosed with tuberculosis. Effective treatment for the disease was still a decade away, and the stricken seventeen-year-old took the news as a death sentence. He spent the next five months in bed.

> I felt death pulling at me time and time again in my terrible suffering and pain. Grieving over my plight, night after night my mother whispered in my ear, "Oral, God is not going to let the devil kill you. You were born to preach the gospel, as your father has done, and someday pray for the sick, as I've done."
>
> All this sounded so far away, so strange. I lay five months hovering between life and death. I could feel nothing inside me responding to God until my sister, Jewel, came to my bedside and said seven words that changed my life forever: "Oral, God is going to heal you."
>
> A loving God had heard both my parents' prayers and sought to honor them. My conversion now came quickly, for my heart had been touched by a power I had not personally known.[37]

Oral Roberts would be healed of both tuberculosis and a stuttering tongue just a few weeks later when his older brother, Elmer, who was not a practicing believer, nonetheless insisted on taking him to a revival meeting in a nearby town.

> When we made it to the service, the minister anointed me with oil and prayed a prayer, the words of which seemed to penetrate every fiber of my being: "You foul, tormenting disease, I command you in the name of Jesus Christ of Nazareth, you come out of this young man. Loose him and let him go free!"

I felt healing instantly in both my lungs and in my speech, but it took months to recover my strength and to realize I was actually free from a stuttering tongue and that I was *called to preach the gospel*.[38]

Oral Roberts's mother spoke hope over her son before he was born, never wavering in her profession, even when he lay dying before her eyes. His older sister, Jewel, having heard that profession hold steady for seventeen rocky years, spoke words of hope over her brother. Even Elmer exercised true faith for his kid brother, because that faith had been awakened by Claudia's constant words of hope.

Many parents don't realize the sway that even the most casually spoken words hold over their children, especially in the early years. My own mother remembers how, when she was only five, one little sentence from her dad made an impact on her that has lasted into her nineties.

"One day my dad misplaced something," she recalls, "and both he and my mother searched for it for a long time to no avail. Then I heard him tell Mum, 'Go ask Ann to look. She can find anything.' From that moment on, I *was* that girl, and to this day I find a certain pride in being able to locate what other people have lost."

A man wields pure spiritual might when he tells his wife she's beautiful or hugs his daughter and praises her purity and innocence. In fact, daughters are far more likely to hold on to their innocence in order to hold on to Daddy's praises. The important thing, in every case, is to praise loved ones for who they are and for the gifts of God you see in them.

- "It's such a pleasure to hear you praying over our children, honey."

- "You're such a good helper to your mom in the kitchen."
- "You played hard out there on the field today, son. I'm proud of you."
- "Go ask Ann. She can find anything."

I was thirty-four years old before I ever heard my father say, "I love you." I was preparing to leave for South Africa with Living Sound and had stopped by my folks' little mobile home in Minneapolis to say good-bye. Dad walked over, hugged me, and said, "I'm proud of you, son. I love you."

> *Many parents don't realize the sway that even the most casually spoken words hold over their children, especially in the early years.*

That moment is perfectly framed in my memory: I can still see the spot where we stood in the living area and how its velvety, red wallpaper—probably even redder in my memory—differentiated it from the kitchen. And I vividly recall the tears coursing down Dad's weathered cheeks.

I had needed to hear those words all my life, but Dad was as much a Canadian farmer as he was a preacher. He just didn't talk that way. As a result, I grew up always trying to earn his approval. If I brought home five As and a B on my report card, he would point to the B and reply with an icy "You can do better." If I brought home all As, he would say nothing. Even when I graduated summa cum laude from Oral Roberts University, there had been no response.

Standing there in Dad's living room in Minneapolis, I felt a void of thirty-four years being filled at last. To this day, those three little words are a greater treasure to me than any degree, and they undoubtedly rank right up with the greatest adventures I've ever experienced. I have replayed them again and again during difficult times and have always found myself reinvigorated and renewed in confidence.

- "I choose not to participate in the recession."
- "Go ask Ann. She can find anything."
- "I love you, son."
- "You are—you shall be."

This is the voice of hope.

8

THE PROMISES OF HOPE

For whatever was written in earlier times was written for our instruction, so that through perseverance and the encouragement of the Scriptures we might have hope.[1]

—St. Paul

Ａfter Jesus's crucifixion, Mary Magdalene and certain other "women who had come with Him out of Galilee" gathered on Good Friday afternoon to prepare spices and perfumes for the slain Savior's body.[2] Then, after resting on the Sabbath, as the law prescribed, they arose at first light on Sunday and made their way to the tomb, only to discover its stone door rolled aside and the body of Jesus missing, with only His burial garments remaining. It must have been a shocking moment, especially on the heels of having seen their one true hope nailed to a Roman cross. But that was just the beginning. Suddenly, two men clothed in dazzling robes appeared and spoke to them, amplifying their fright all the more. The women bowed low, too terrified to look into the faces of what were obviously angelic beings.

"Why do you seek the living One among the dead?" the angels asked. "He is not here, but He has risen. Remember how He spoke to you while He was still in Galilee, saying that the Son of Man must be delivered into the hands of sinful men, and be crucified, and the third day rise again."[3]

It was a short but effective sermon: "And they remembered His words."[4] That's a short but monumentally important sentence. Jesus had indeed told His disciples sometime earlier about all of the events that would transpire on this terrible weekend, but at the time they had failed to grasp what He was saying.[5] Now, the women remembered the Lord's words and hurried back to tell the rest of His forlorn followers what had just happened. Unfortunately, the majority still didn't understand, dismissing their report as "nonsense, and they would not believe them."[6]

Shortly thereafter, two of the Lord's disheartened followers left Jerusalem for the village of Emmaus seven miles away. As they walked, they were discussing Jesus's death—and no doubt the quickly spreading rumor of His resurrection—when the Savior appeared nearby and began walking with them, "but their eyes were prevented from recognizing Him."[7] Obviously, the Lord could have easily revealed His identity to the men, but He chose a different tack, one that would prove to be far more beneficial to them—and to you.

THE IMPORTANCE OF BEING EARNEST

First, He asked them what they were discussing, not because He didn't already know but in order to get them to express the disappointment that had overwhelmed them. "It's about Jesus the Nazarene," they began, describing Him as "a prophet mighty in deed and word in the sight of God and all the people."

Then the two disciples got to the point: "But *we were hoping* that it was He who was going to redeem Israel." The "we" in that statement was a lot bigger than these two men and their band of disenchanted colleagues back in Jerusalem. Centuries earlier God had promised Israel a Messiah (literally "Anointed One") who would fulfill the prophecy to Abraham that his "seed" would multiply and fill the earth with blessing.[8] The whole nation had been awaiting Him ever since. Sadly, however, virtually all of the Jews misunderstood the nature of Israel's redemption. Since they had spent much of their existence as a nation in political bondage to various foreign powers, from ancient Egypt to their current occupier, Rome, they thought the Messianic kingdom would be political in nature. That's why the crowd in Luke 19 had assumed that, since Jesus was nearing Jerusalem, the kingdom of God was going to "appear immediately."[9]

Even the Lord's closest disciples had been caught up in this thinking, going so far as to argue about their respective spots in the pecking order of His future kingdom.[10] And because Israel didn't understand the nature of the kingdom of God, they had been unable to recognize their King when He came to them. Indeed, He had been crucified for announcing His reign.

"But we were hoping that it was He who was going to redeem Israel." That was honest disappointment and exactly what Jesus wanted to hear the men say. He wanted them to put everything on the table so He could heal them and give them *true* hope.

Keeping Hope Alive

Jesus could have revealed Himself to these two disciples in the same way He would show Himself to the whole group a few hours later, by appearing out of thin air and showing them the nail prints on His hands and feet. But He chose a different course: *He revealed Himself to them in the same way He reveals Himself to you and me.*

"Then beginning with Moses and with all the prophets, He explained to them the things concerning Himself in *all the Scriptures.*"[11]

Isn't it fascinating that these two men, like the majority of their fellow Israelites, were very religious, quite dedicated to their national heritage, and had heard the Word of God all their lives, yet still failed to understand? So Jesus went back fourteen hundred years, all the way to the prophetic writings of Moses, and began showing them what you and I need to see: *the whole Bible is about life in Jesus.* All of it.

In Genesis, when God promised Abraham that, "in your seed all the nations of the earth shall be blessed,"[12] He was talking about Jesus and by extension those of us who have been "born again not of seed which is perishable but imperishable, that is, through the living and enduring word of God."[13]

In the Psalms, when King David lamented, "For dogs have surrounded Me; the congregation of the wicked has enclosed Me. They pierced My hands and My feet; I can count all My bones. They look and stare at Me. They divide My garments among them, and for My clothing they cast lots,"[14] he clearly was not talking about himself. He was prophesying about the coming Messiah, Jesus of Nazareth, when He hung on the cross.

David's words are astounding in their accuracy, as are the lyrics of one of his other prophetic laments: "Reproach has broken my heart and I am so sick. And I looked for sympathy, but there was none, and for comforters, but I found none. They also gave me gall for my food and for my thirst they gave me vinegar to drink."[15] If you've ever read Matthew 27:34–35 or seen its very faithful portrayal in the movie *The Passion of the Christ*, you know that Jesus's tormentors fulfilled David's words to the last letter.

Isaiah had also heard the voice of Jesus, hundreds of years in advance, when he wrote, "I gave My back to those who strike Me, and My cheeks to those who pluck out the beard; I did not cover My face from humiliation and spitting."[16] Isaiah never suffered that abuse, but Jesus did.

> *God gave us prophets to give us promises and promises to give us hope.*

How could Moses, David, and Isaiah—among others—prophesy with such precision about Jesus and His sufferings? St. Peter explained that "the prophets who prophesied of the grace that would come to you made careful searches and inquiries, seeking to know what person or time *the Spirit of Christ within them* was indicating as He predicted the sufferings of Christ and the glories to follow."[17] And why did God give the prophets such messages? Peter continues: "It was revealed to them that they were not serving themselves, but you."[18] Got that? The prophets were not serving themselves; they were serving *you*! Everything they wrote was to encourage you, to give you hope in someone greater than your circumstances.

That is why St. Peter's very next words are so encouraging: "Therefore, prepare your minds for action, keep sober in spirit, fix your hope completely on the grace to be brought to you at the revelation of Jesus Christ."[19] Peter was saying that because God gave the prophets their astounding messages for you, you thereby have every right to get your hopes up because of what they said.

This advance witness of the Old Testament prophets is

key to your hope. They were a diverse group whose writings spanned centuries. Yet together they perfectly predicted the circumstances and events of Jesus's life, death, and resurrection.[20] That fact, more than any other, is the primary proof that the Bible really is God's Word. It is why phrases like "so that the Scripture would be fulfilled" and "according to the Scriptures" appear so often in New Testament accounts of the Lord's ministry. In 1 Corinthians 15, St. Paul even placed Jesus's fulfillment of prophecy ahead of eyewitness accounts. He knew that the true power of the gospel comes from God's Word.

Jesus had repeatedly rebutted Satan's temptations in the wilderness by citing what the prophets had said concerning Him. He Himself drew strength from His Father's Word, and on the road to Emmaus He wanted these discouraged, dejected disciples to know that the promises of God were key to their hopes as well.

> *Hope stirs faith the way the sight of the finish line stirs the runner.*

"Were not our hearts burning within us while He was speaking to us on the road, while He was explaining the Scriptures to us?" the two men asked themselves rhetorically. Jesus had achieved His objective. Their hope had been extinguished three days earlier, and now He had set that hope on fire again. Mission accomplished. But note that He achieved it not with an emotional appeal but simply by unfolding what God's Word had said all along.

That Word still has not changed. It is filled with the messages of the prophets, every one of whom was God's instrument to point you and me to Jesus. They simply wrote "as they were carried along by the Holy Spirit."[21] Jesus, in turn, sent His Holy Spirit, promising that "He will guide you into all the truth."[22] In a nutshell: *God gave us prophets to give us promises and promises to give us hope.* The Bible is the complete compilation of those promises and is given to us that we might have hope in an otherwise hopeless world. Our faith will never know fulfillment without it, because hope precedes faith and gives it focus. Hope stirs faith the way the sight of the finish line stirs the runner.

Promises, Promises

Of course, a promise is only as good as the person making it. That's why you put more stock in people you know than in those you don't know. When someone you know to be a person of character makes a promise, you can rest assured that he or she will make good on it. But when the guy with the toothy grin and plaid sports coat says he's giving you a "special price" on that new car, you want to check his word against a reliable consumer magazine, don't you? You can only trust the promise if you trust the person, and you cannot trust someone you do not know. That is why the Jews in Jesus's day failed to understand God's promises about the Messiah and why, even today, many men and women with seminary degrees still fail to grasp the promises of God. They have never gotten to know Him, so His words are as incomprehensible to them as the women's news of Jesus's resurrection was to His disciples.

The Bible explains that "whatever was written in earlier times was written for our instruction, so that through perseverance and the encouragement of the Scriptures we might have hope."[23] Jesus spent several hours giving "the encouragement of the Scriptures" to His audience of two on the road to Emmaus, because He wanted to give them a truer, more reliable hope than they had known before. But this kind of hope doesn't come from visions or miracles—they had seen plenty over the past three years. No, real hope comes from digging into the living Word of God and treasuring it in your heart. Only later, when Jesus ate a meal with them, did the Lord open the men's eyes to recognize Him. Then, almost immediately, He vanished from their sight. At that point, they no longer needed to "see" Him in person. Now they could see Him in His Word.

> *Real hope comes from digging into the living Word of God and treasuring it in your heart.*

WHEN HOPE WAS BORN

If you ask me to zoom in on one crystalline moment in history when hope was born for you and me, it has to be when God spoke to an elderly man named Abram, renamed him Abraham[24] because he was going to father a great nation, and promised him that "in you all the families of the earth will be blessed."[25] Author Lewis Smedes beautifully reimagines the scene from Genesis 12.

> Sometime, in the dead of night perhaps, Abraham heard a voice, heard it with an inner ear that no sound waves ever touched, but heard it with a clarity that no one who heard it could question.
>
> "Go," the Voice said. "Take Sarah and go."
>
> "Go where?"
>
> "Never mind. You will find out when you get there."
>
> "But why?"

"Because I have chosen you to be the father of a new nation that will bless all the peoples of all the world."

Abraham, as far as we know, had never heard the Voice before. The Voice could have been no more than a rumble from his own soul. But Abraham knew that it was a real voice he heard, and he knew whose Voice it was. How did he *know* that he knew?

I have sometimes wondered what Sarah was thinking when she woke up before dawn and found her husband bustling about in the shadows with his foremen, loading down his pack animals and getting his flocks arranged for a long trek across the fertile crescent to the other side of his world.

"What in the world are you up to, my husband?"

"Packing, as you can see."

"Where are we going?"

"I don't know."

"But why are we going?"

"He told me to."

"Who's He?"

"God."

"How do you know it was God?"

"He spoke to me in a dream."

"Perhaps my husband only dreamed that God spoke to him."

"Good wife, when God talks to you, you *know* that it is God who is talking to you."

…So that same morning Abraham led a compliant but worried Sarah by the hand and walked with her into the desert toward a place they could barely imagine and into a future that they could not at all

control. Thus began the odyssey of hope for the father
and mother of all who put their hope in God.[26]

Abraham's friends and relatives must have thought the old
gentleman had turned senile. First, here he was, seventy-five
years old, uprooting his household because God told him to
do so. Second, God had said his sixty-five-year-old wife was
going to bear a son. But everyone knew that Sarah had been
barren for years. Third, from this one son an entire nation
would be born, and the whole world would be blessed as a
result. It was all so preposterous—the old guy *must* be off his
rocker, especially since he claimed God was talking to him.

I find it interesting that in today's culture you can talk
to God all you want and it's OK. But if He talks back—well,
suddenly you're crazy, arrogant, or evil, if not all three!
Unless, of course, He really *has* spoken to you. If that were
the case, then how could you *not* obey His command? As
Smedes observes, "No one to whom God has surely spoken is
open to rational alternatives."[27] Abraham knew he had heard
God, so it no longer mattered what his relatives and neighbors
thought. The world could call him crazy if they wished, but
his experience with God proved he wasn't.

> *If Abraham had to hope against hope, so*
> *Jesus had to hope against hell, because*
> *that was the only way for hope—yours and*
> *mine—to rise immortal three days later.*

Abraham would have plenty of time to look back and
remember that night, and plenty of time to question the experience, because another twenty-five years would pass before
he saw God's promise fulfilled. Why did the Almighty wait
so long to bring it to pass? *Because He wanted Abraham to*

have no hope other than the promise. Sarah was barren when the Lord had first spoken to Abraham, but he himself was still quite capable of fathering a child. So the Lord waited until Abraham was also "as good as dead."[28] At that point, says the apostle Paul, "In hope against hope he believed, so that he might become a father of many nations according to that which had been spoken, 'So shall your descendants be.'"[29]

"In hope against hope he believed." No statement could better summarize Abraham's twenty-five-year journey from the improbable, through the impossible, to the incredible: the birth of Isaac, father of Jacob, father of the twelve tribes of Israel.

But Israel is only one nation, and the Lord told Abraham that He would make him the "father of many nations."[30] How did that part of the promise come to pass? Abraham's "hope against hope" was the *spiritual seed* that gave birth to his faith for the impossible. And just as his physical seed made him the father of one nation through the birth of Isaac, hope's spiritual seed made him the father of many nations through faith in the death and resurrection of Jesus.

WHEN HOPE WAS BORN AGAIN

As I pointed out in chapter 2, Christianity hinges upon the resurrection of Jesus from the dead. If He isn't alive, "then our preaching is vain, your faith also is vain."[31] That is why, on the Day of Pentecost, St. Peter's preaching centered on the resurrection of Jesus and in particular on one of King David's prophetic psalms.

> For David says of Him, "I saw the Lord always in my presence; for He is at my right hand, so that I will not be shaken. Therefore my heart was glad and my tongue exulted; *moreover my flesh also will live*

117

> *in hope*; because You will not abandon my soul to
> Hades, nor allow your Holy One to undergo decay.
> You have made known to me the ways of life; You
> will make me full of gladness with your presence."[32]

King David was not the "Holy One" in this passage. He was prophetically speaking the words of Jesus as He agonized before God on the cross. By that time the Lord had already endured unimaginable suffering, starting in the Garden of Gethsemane, when the strain of what He was facing caused Him to sweat drops of blood. Then the horrors had intensified when the Roman soldiers beat Him, pierced His brow with a crown of thorns, lashed open the flesh on His back, and nailed His hands and feet to the cross upon which He now hung. Yet He knew that even this was not the culmination of His passion but only its beginning. He knew that soon He would surrender His body in death and then descend into the very belly of hell. Satisfying His Father's wrath against sin and securing the world's redemption required no less.

But Jesus also knew something else. He knew His Father's *promise*, and He clung to it. "Moreover my flesh also will live in hope, because You will not abandon my soul to Hades, nor allow your Holy One to undergo decay." Even as He stared at the gaping jaws of death, *Jesus hoped in the promise of God.* He put His life, His body, and His future in God's hands; gave up the ghost; and went to hell, taking all of our hopes with Him. The hope that had been born with Abraham died with Jesus. But then, it *had* to. For if Abraham had to hope against hope, so Jesus had to hope against hell, because that was the only way for hope—yours and mine—to rise immortal three days later.

OUT ON A LIMB

"After two millennia, there is one sign that keeps telling us that God has what it takes to make good on His promise," says Lewis Smedes.[33]

> It is that baffling but wondrous thing that happened one early morning as the fingers of the day's early light were filtering through the floor of a burial garden in Jerusalem. The thing that happened when the life-birthing energy of the universe's Maker began to pulse inside the dead biological remains of the buried Jesus, whom God had apparently abandoned two [*sic*] days before. The cells regenerated themselves, and He, body and soul, came back to life.
>
> Any rational skeptic will remind me that ancient rumors of a rabbi's resurrection make a thin limb on which to hang the hopes of the world. Yes, I would admit it's a thin limb, but sturdy enough for all, that to have held up a sign for all these ages that God the Creator has the competence to renew the world He made.[34]

This is our hope: The prophets were right. God's Word is true. Jesus died for our sins and was raised from the dead for our justification. The kingdoms of this world belong to Him. He reigns on high and will continue to reign until all His enemies, including death, have become His footstool. Then He will come. Death will die. We will live. The Prince of Peace will reign, and we will reign with Him forever.

Jesus hoped in the promise of God.

How do I know? Because *He promised.*

THE HELMET OF HOPE

After victory, tighten your helmet strap.
—JAPANESE PROVERB

W OULD YOU RIDE a motorcycle without wearing a helmet? It's amazing how many riders do, even though in crashes they are three times more likely to suffer traumatic brain injuries—*if* they survive—than helmeted riders.[1] One Florida surgeon told my coauthor, "When our state law changed to allow riding without a helmet, my business actually went down rather than up. Dead people don't need surgery."

Unlike Florida, the Bible has a helmet law. It is part of a larger provision, a suit of armor that God has given to every Christian as a means of defense, since we are all under constant attack by the accuser.[2] In addition to the offensive weapons of His Word, Jesus's name, and His blood,[3] God has outfitted us with several pieces of defensive armor, including a belt of truth, breastplate of righteousness, shoes of the preparation of peace, shield of faith, helmet of salvation, and the sword of the Spirit, which is God's Word.[4]

Hope, more than anything else, has to do with the helmet.

In 1 Thessalonians 5:8, St. Paul calls it the helmet of "the *hope* of salvation." This helmet law isn't about to be repealed, but it won't be enforced against your will either. It is *your* helmet, and *you must put it on.* Just because you've committed your life to Christ doesn't mean that you automatically have your armor in place. *You must choose to suit up* if you're going to withstand the fiery arrows aimed at you by Satan.

> *You must choose to build up your hope, just as surely as you choose to build up your faith and deepen your love.*

At first, the term "helmet of salvation" sounds very generic, since most believers think getting "saved" is something like being rescued by a lifeguard: it happens, you're thankful, and it's history. But salvation is really an ongoing, unfolding reality, like marriage. Yes, you "get married," and thereafter you can say you and your spouse *were* married on such and such a date. But just as you continue being married, you also continue being saved.

Likewise, your helmet of "the hope of salvation" is something you rely on for continuous protection. That is why the Bible's famous love chapter refers to faith, hope, and love as *abiding* realities.[5] They aren't gifts you receive and then stash in a drawer somewhere like keepsakes. You must build your faith, hope, and love. Love and faith certainly are taught this way, in sermon after sermon and book after book, to such an extent that more than a few speaking and writing careers have been based on them. Yet, until recently, hope has been the forgotten virtue. Over the past thirty-five years I can recall hearing only one sermon on hope, even though Romans 15:13 calls our Lord "the God of hope." But you must choose to build up your hope, just as surely as you choose to build up your faith and deepen your love.

No wonder so many Christians suffer chronic depression, their lives filled with worry, fear, pessimism, and cynicism. Their minds have been left unprotected, because they have never chosen to put on their helmets and build up their hope. Faith and love are wonderful, but without hope your armor is incomplete; *you need all three to be fully protected.*

THOUGHT ATTACK

The mind is Satan's point of access to human beings, the place where he conducts what I call "thought attacks."[6] That is why he has made himself an expert in diverse systems of thought, such as communism and Islam, as well as other more subtle but no less insidious obsessions, such as America's relentless pursuit of amusement, pleasure, and leisure as the ultimate goals of life. As we shall see below, St. Paul refers to such mental constructs as satanic "strongholds" and claims that God has given us spiritual weapons to protect us from their onslaught.

This comes as a surprise to many Christians who don't believe the adversary has access to their minds, but he does. We are under constant attack every day—especially via TV, movies, and the Internet—with sex, violence, alcohol, drugs, rebellion, eating disorders, self-mutilation, and more. The sins of the twenty-first century have been "mainstreamed." They are such a way of life that most people don't even recognize them. Indeed, the sworn enemy of our souls is able to wreak havoc largely because most people don't believe he exists. Even many Christians think he's just a cartoon metaphor for evil.

I read a report not long ago that claimed that 80 percent of our thoughts come from our five senses: sight, hearing, touch, taste, and smell, with another 10 percent arising from memories triggered by present events. But the Bible indicates that many of our thoughts come straight from another source: the spiritual realm, specifically from God or from the devil. God speaks both to the spirit and mind, and He does so on a regular basis. But the accuser approaches us through our thoughts; that is his primary method of tempting you and me. *Satan wants to convince you that all of your thoughts originate with you.* That way you'll keep on condemning yourself, telling yourself that you don't have the power to change.

> *Faith and love are wonderful, but without hope your armor is incomplete; you need all three to be fully protected.*

His strategy has never varied from the time he approached Adam and Eve. "Did God actually say...?" the tempter probed, and they took the bait. In fact, for several millennia such "suggestions" trapped victim after victim. But the ruse was finally exposed when Jesus, recognizing Satan in the desert, shot back with, "It is written..." That is why the Bible says Jesus returned from the wilderness "in the power of the Spirit."[7] He had used the Word against the tempter, and the tempter had to withdraw.

If you don't believe this battlefield scenario, then take a look at what Paul, Peter, John, Luke, and Jesus Himself had to say on the subject.

We're in a real spiritual war:

> For our struggle is not against flesh and blood, but against the rulers, against the powers, against the world forces of this darkness, against the spiritual forces of wickedness in the heavenly places.
> —EPHESIANS 6:12

The devil blinds people morally:

> The god of this world has blinded the minds of the
> unbelieving so that they might not see the light of
> the gospel of the glory of Christ, who is the image
> of God.
>
> —2 CORINTHIANS 4:4

He holds their minds captive:

> [If perhaps] they may come to their senses and escape
> from the snare of the devil, having been held captive
> by him to do his will.
>
> —2 TIMOTHY 2:26

After gaining a foothold in the mind, he builds a fortress:

> For the weapons of our warfare are not of the
> flesh, but divinely powerful for the destruction of
> fortresses. We are destroying speculations and every
> lofty thing raised up against the knowledge of God,
> and we are taking every thought captive to the obedi-
> ence of Christ.
>
> —2 CORINTHIANS 10:4–5

After securing the mind, he goes for the heart:

> But Peter said, "Ananias, why has Satan filled your
> heart to lie to the Holy Spirit and to keep back some
> of the price of the land?"
>
> —ACTS 5:3

Everyone is either in the grip of God or the snare of Satan:

> We know that we are held firm by God; it's only the people of the world who continue in the grip of the Evil One.
>
> —1 John 5:19, The Message

The Path to Bondage

> But I am afraid that, as the serpent deceived Eve by his craftiness, your minds will be led astray from the simplicity and purity of devotion to Christ.
>
> —2 Corinthians 11:3

Satan's strategy is to rob you of simple, pure hope in God by replacing it with false hopes in everything but God. Then your life gets very complicated as you chase the illusions the adversary dangles in front of you. Satisfaction is always just beyond reach, always waiting in one more drink, one more affair, one more roll of the dice. Author David Augsburger vividly describes the futility born of false hope:

> As long as there is hope, the addict will pursue his addiction. The drug dependent will cling to the bottle, needle, or powder...the rescuing spouse will cover for the alcoholic, tolerate the irritation and abuse, bend the schedule, break the budget, ruin the family plans to adjust to his bender. The hope is irresistible, that the most recent promise will be kept, that this new apology will prove genuine, that the latest pledge to go dry will be the last....
>
> As long as there is hope, the grownup child will continue to search for the rejecting parent. Hope

induces the person to keep calling for the father to come and give love, even long after he's dead....

As long as there is hope, the Don Juan will dream of a more desirable lover, pursue a more exciting liaison, seek conquest after conquest. It is hope that lures the woman to look for affection or infatuation outside her covenant of marriage. Perhaps the next lover will have the magic, the mystery, the magnetism that will satisfy her emptiness.

...In time, hope fades. The highs no longer seem high enough or are too hard to reach. The lows linger longer and leave a residue of despair.[8]

Strongholds like addiction, codependency, rejection, and lust aren't established overnight. Each begins with a single thought. Then a thought entertained becomes a fantasy, a fantasy an obsession, an obsession an addiction. The destruction of a stronghold is similar: it must be torn down brick by brick—thought by thought.

> *Repentance doesn't mean simply saying, "I'm sorry." Repentance is all about the way you decide to think.*

Just stopping isn't enough. You can't fight something with nothing and claim a spiritual victory. Strongholds have to be torn down and *replaced*. In other words, ungodly thought systems must be replaced by godly thought systems. But how is this done?

The Power of Repentance

When Jesus preached His first sermon, He came straight to the point: "Repent and believe in the gospel."[9] In today's English He was saying, "Change your *way of thinking* and fill your heart and mind with the good news."

After former President Bill Clinton appeared on national television to finally confess to a sexual dalliance with a White House intern, network commentators on the political Left and Right debated whether or not he had expressed repentance. While Mr. Clinton's carefully parsed phrases no doubt had clouded the issue, one fact was crystalline: nobody seemed capable of defining what the word *repent* actually meant.

Repentance doesn't mean simply saying, "I'm sorry," nor does it necessarily require deep emotion. *Repentance is all about the way you decide to think.* It involves cleansing your mind with what the Bible calls "the washing of water with the word."[10] As you fill your mind with God's thoughts, you simultaneously cleanse it of all matter of unholy clutter. Nobody I know personifies the power of repentance better than a young woman named Gretchen, who lives on the West Coast. My wife Barbara first read about her on the Internet, and then we called her to ask permission to relate portions of her story to you.

Gretchen began reading romance novels when she was about nine years old and quickly developed a fixation about being attractive to men. She also became obsessed with being liked at school. At fourteen she experienced her first intimate relationship with a boy and, not coincidentally, developed an eating disorder. A series of unhealthy relationships followed, and by her junior year in high school Gretchen was living in the fast lane, drinking, using drugs, and suffering from full-blown bulimia.

"Marijuana made me want to eat and sleep," she says. Additionally, as she binged more, she also purged more. The cycle accelerated until, "in a hysterical moment I finally confided in my mom and told her I wanted to get some counseling. My parents did what they could to find the best psychologist in the area, and I saw him weekly until I left for college two years later." But there her habit only worsened.

> I taught myself to purge after a binge by sticking a long eye-shadow pencil down my throat. I soon developed a pattern of driving to several stores, bakeries, and fast-food joints over a period of a couple hours, eating between stops, going home and finishing what I could, and then throwing it all up.[11]

Gretchen's addiction dragged her from a 4.0 freshman average to failing every class by the time she dropped out of college during her senior year. "I was bingeing and purging on the average of three times a day and was chronically depressed," she says. Frantic for help, she returned for a while to psychological counseling, including Christian counseling, "which seemed smarter at the time but really left me no better."

Eventually Gretchen searched out a good church and a helpful pastor. Yet even after experiencing the joy of being born again, she still found herself bound by the stronghold of bulimia. Now a practicing Christian, yet unable to find relief, she was utterly bereft of self-confidence. That low point was where the healing she craved finally began to take place.

> I was devouring the Word of God.... I loved hearing, reading, and talking about God, and my husband and I went to church nearly as often as the doors were opened.... Much of the damage in my life was repaired, simply by the power of the Holy Spirit working in me as I continued to put myself in a

position to receive from God. My mind cleared, and my emotions became increasingly stable. I began to get a revelation of what real beauty is, and the bleached hair, long nails, and suggestive clothing went by the wayside. It just seemed the natural way to go....

But the sin of gluttony isn't about weight or fat. It's about eating too much. It's about indulgence and lust and selfishness. And I knew I had plenty of that going on in my life.[12]

The key for Gretchen wasn't to stop sinning—she had failed at that—but to start doing the opposite. That's what the word *repent* means: *it's an inner change of mind resulting in an outward change of direction.* So Gretchen began feasting—*bingeing*—on the Word of God, taking it to heart just as King David said: "Your word I have treasured in my heart, that I may not sin against You."[13]

> *If God's Word diagnoses your condition as sin and commands you to repent, then you are empowered by the very command to obey it.*

"The Word is *different* from any other book you can ever read," she says, "*living and active.*"[14] Today Gretchen counsels others with eating disorders, and maintains a Web site called "Renovation."[15] The advice she gives is just as powerful as her story.

People with eating disorders and those who treat them have forever been trying to place the blame somewhere typically outside the person with the disorder.

We want to believe that our problem happens to us rather than in us. Society loves and adores the victim model. Commonly, we are taught to blame our problematic behaviors on negative life experiences and the people who contributed to them, or on disease, or even on genetics. Personal responsibility is not too popular a concept in most circles.

...I know it is extremely hard to hear and even harder to accept, but an eating disorder is a chosen lifestyle. Just as everyone possesses a carnal or sinful nature from birth, so also do we come into this world with a free will. Most people don't really realize just how free they are to choose. The fact is, much of what we feel victimized by, we actually played a huge part in bringing on ourselves because of choices we have made....

The characteristic that is common to all eating disorders is the feeling of helplessness. Yet, in actuality, an eating disorder is the cumulative effect of a series of choices. People do, in fact, get to a point where the ability to choose seems completely spent. But originally, choices were available, and choices were made....

When the Lord began healing me emotionally and my life was getting better and better and as many of my excuses for overeating were gone, I remember well how startling it was to discover that one big reason I overate was because I wanted to eat.[16]

Gretchen faced her sin for what it was, accepted responsibility, and discovered the liberating power of repentance. If someone tells you that you're psychologically sick or that your "condition" is genetic, then by accepting that diagnosis you surrender hope. It's out of your hands. But if God's Word diagnoses your condition as sin and commands you to repent, then you are *empowered by* the very command to obey it. This is because God's Word really is alive; it isn't just something He once said, but it's what He is still saying *now*. That's exactly why 1 Thessalonians 5:24 says, "Faithful is He who calls you, and He also will bring it to pass." *The command to obey always includes the power to obey.*

REPENTANCE LEADS TO HOPE

You might say you've repented in the past but it didn't work. If so, then you probably are confusing repentance with remorse. Satan hates repentance because it renders him powerless, but he loves remorse because it is something he can amplify with accusations. That was the case with Judas after he had betrayed Jesus. He felt so bad that he tried to give back the bribe he had accepted. But where true repentance would have driven him to his knees to ask for mercy, remorse drove him to commit suicide. That is precisely what St. Paul meant when he said, "For the sorrow that is according to the will of God produces a repentance without regret, leading to salvation, but the sorrow of the world produces death."[17]

> *"Next to life itself, the power to choose is your greatest gift." —Stephen Covey*

What is the difference between godly sorrow and worldly sorrow, between repentance and remorse? Hope! The hope of God's mercy is the power—the engine—that drives true repentance. And the only way to "find" such hope is to *choose* it. *Remorse is just a feeling, but repentance is a choice.*

As I have noted elsewhere, world-renowned leadership consultant Stephen Covey calls our freedom to choose the "one great idea [that resonates] deeper in the soul than any other" and is what his audiences find "most practical, most relevant, most timely, regardless of circumstances....Next to life itself, the power to choose is your greatest gift. This power and freedom stand in stark contrast to the mind-set of *victimism* and culture of *blame* so prevalent in society today."[18] Covey is right. Political correctness insists on deflecting blame and denying guilt, claiming instead that people are simply the victims of their upbringing or casualties of their culture. All they *really* need is more education. They think that by denying man's sin they restore his innocence, but in reality they are robbing him of hope.

Blame shifting is the driving force behind political correctness and its philosophical sibling, radical environmentalism. Both are subsets of a larger worldview that claims man's problems are not internal but external or environmental. This concept finds widespread acceptance because it is preferable to recognizing human responsibility and the need for repentance, which would require admitting that man's problem is actually an *internal* thing called sin.

Admitting to sin explains why evil exists in the world, but it also squelches all human excuses. Thus most societies find any other explanation preferable. Young Muslims riot in the streets of Paris? Blame it on a lack of economic opportunity. Illegitimacy rates skyrocket in our cities? Poverty and a lack of education are the culprits. A teenager shoots up his school, killing his teacher and several students? Must be insanity, says a psychologist. Bring in trained grief counselors, but don't let local pastors come in; they might claim that sin caused a normal person to commit unspeakable evil.

"But that's impossible!" society cries. It makes the killer too much like us, as though we all have such a capacity. The truth is, such depravity may be impossible to comprehend, but it's not impossible to commit. As young Jeremiah said long ago, "The heart is more deceitful than all else and is desperately sick; who can understand it?"[19] Sin may be an ugly truth, but it is real, and admitting to its existence makes repentance possible. Repentance, in turn, makes hope possible.

As we said earlier, sin did not originate with man and was not natural to him as God's creation. That is why we refer to his *fallen* nature. No, sin came from Satan, whom the Bible describes as an "anointed cherub" in whom "unrighteousness was *found*."[20] That unrighteousness was transmitted to humanity when Adam and Eve chose to entertain and then act on the devil's suggestion to rebel. The first family suffered history's first thought attack. Satan had not aimed at their hearts but at their heads.

> *Admitting to sin explains why evil exists in the world, but it also squelches all human excuses.*

THE HELMET OF HOPE

U.S. Army Specialist Adrian Danczyk knows the importance of a good helmet. On November 8, 2003, in a firefight near Fallujah, Iraq, he took a machine gun bullet front and center above the eyes and lived to tell about it. Why? Because he happened to be field-testing the Army's new advanced combat helmet, whose layers of polymer fiber absorbed the round. Instead of literally losing his head, Danczyk required only two stitches where the helmet's inner shell had punched his forehead. The young man, who plans to make the army his career, says he'll "never, ever" allow his soldiers into battle without the helmet that saved his life.[21]

The helmet Adrian Danczyk wore is designed to absorb the impact of a 9-millimeter bullet fired at close range. But the helmet of hope will guard you against an attack even more deadly that bullets: "But since we are of the day, let us be sober, having put on the breastplate of faith and love, and as a helmet, the hope of salvation."[22] Here is God's advanced combat helmet, specifically designed to protect your mind from Satan's thought attacks. Unlike Danczyk's headgear, however, the helmet of hope never needs replacing and is actually strengthened rather than weakened when attacked. Furthermore, it not only protects its wearer from new wounds, but also it even heals the scars of battles past.

In these pages, I have repeatedly defined hope as "the confident expectation of the goodness of God" because I want that concept to permeate your thinking. I want you to come to the point in life where you would never think of walking out the door in the morning without first putting on your helmet of hope, as I endeavor to do every day.

I remind myself that "God causes all things to work together for good to those who love God, to those who are called according to His purpose."[23] How can you say those words and remain pessimistic or downcast?

When I fly into Baghdad and the pilot puts our plane into a steep, corkscrew descent to dodge enemy rockets, I quote King David's words: "Surely goodness and mercy shall follow me all the days of my life; and I will dwell in the house of the LORD forever."[24] Those words fortify me and keep fear from claiming the day.

I have a list of favorite quotes from Scripture, and I keep them on my mind, much like the soldier who keeps a photo of his wife and kids tucked inside his helmet. (See the authors' companion book *Hope Promises*.) For example, there's Matthew 7:11, which says God is a better gift-giver than any earthly father, and James 1:17, which characterizes the gifts of God as good and perfect and headed my way. Likewise, Jeremiah 29:11 says, "For I know the thoughts that I think toward you, says the LORD, thoughts of peace and not of evil, to give you a future and a hope." After more than forty years of globetrotting, I've reached a frequent flier status that includes a few benefits, but none like the promises found in Psalm 103:2–5:

> Bless the LORD, O my soul, and forget not all His benefits: who forgives all your iniquities, who heals all your diseases, who redeems your life from destruction, who crowns you with lovingkindness and tender mercies, who satisfies your mouth with good things, so that your youth is renewed like the eagle's.

I won't give away my age, except to say that the final benefit—renewed youth—has become my favorite!

> *I have a list of favorite quotes from Scripture, and I keep them on my mind.*

Thought attacks are a serious business, as real and deadly as anything physical. That's why you have to be serious about wearing your helmet, God's protection for your mind. When you wake up in the morning, as your mind starts kicking into gear, that is the prime time to put on your helmet of hope. Take some verses, like the ones referenced above, and say them to yourself over and over while you're getting dressed. Then you'll be prepared to face the challenges of the day…and of the age.

THE EYES OF HOPE

Too much sanity may be madness! But maddest of all—to see life as it is and not as it should be.[1]
—DON QUIXOTE, *MAN FROM LA MANCHA*

WHAT DO YOU see when you look at the world around you? Do you see reality or someone else's version of it? Seeing through eyes of hope means looking past the world's perspectives and adopting God's point of view.

Iraqi General Georges Sada had been living in the United States for only two weeks when he came to me quite upset one day. "Terry, your government does not truly govern the people of America," he asserted in his crisp Assyrian accent. "They are controlled by your media." He went on to lament the way our television and print media have hijacked national opinion and how they gradually persuade the public by publishing grim images and reports—day after day, month after month—of war, destruction, death, and, most of all, the unrighteousness of our cause. He also accused them of suppressing any facts that disagree with their own preconceptions. Later, when

Georges wrote his book *Saddam's Secrets* about the late dictator's weapons of mass destruction and how he surreptitiously
moved them from Iraq to Syria,[2] the media reaction proved
his last point correct.

During Easter season of 2006, a mainstream British newspaper interviewed the general and me for two hours. Afterward
the reporter said, "You know, general, I believe everything
you're saying is true, but my paper won't print it. They have
taken an editorial position against Prime Minister [Tony]
Blair, and if they printed this, it would appear as though Mr.
Blair was right in his decision to invade Iraq. And because my
paper doesn't like the prime minister, they will choose not to
print it."

"So, it doesn't matter what the truth is?" I interjected. "They
won't print it?"

"Yes, that's correct," she replied wistfully.

A major American TV network also interviewed General
Sada after hiring him to translate several hours of audiotapes
released by the Pentagon, in which Saddam bragged about his
weapons of mass destruction and the possibility of deploying
them to kill one hundred thousand people in Washington DC.
The network's reporter, a familiar face on the nightly news,
asked Georges what he had heard on the tape. "There was no
mistake," replied the general. "This tape declares definitively
that Saddam had WMDs." The interview did not appear on
the air that evening, nor has it since. It was—in newsroom
lingo—spiked.

> *Today's reality has editors, and if you want
> the real truth, you have to see past them.*

Now let me ask you again: What do you see when you look at the world around you? Do you see reality or only what others choose to show you? The answer should be obvious. As they say in the advertising world, perception is reality. In other words, in marketing—and this includes the marketing of news—it isn't truth that matters so much as people's perception of it. If media outlets continually bombard the public with the perception that America is losing a war, then eventually that becomes the "truth" in the public's collective mind. Forget reality as the troops or even the nationals themselves would portray it. Today's reality has editors, and if you want the real truth, you have to see past them. But how?

Seeing What Isn't There

A friend of mine says that any school history course that doesn't begin with "In the beginning God..." is off on the wrong foot. What he means is that any view of history, language, science, economics, mathematics, or any other subject without God at its core is distorted from the start and will skew all other aspects of reality as well. If God is not at the core, then something else—evolution, for example—will be. That's because none of us are perfectly neutral or objective about the way in which we view the world. All of us start with presuppositions, certain "facts" we assume but cannot prove. In church circles we usually call them "statements of faith."

Scientists buck at the notion that they are not objective, but they are as dedicated as the rest of us to their own presuppositions. For example, when the late celebrity/scientist Carl Sagan opened his book *Cosmos* with the sentence "The Cosmos is all that is or ever was or ever will be,"[3] he was making a claim he could not prove. He had neither traveled to the edge of the universe, nor had he touched the past and future boundaries of time. Rather, he made that statement in *blind faith* and then based his whole book, if not his career, on it.

Christians assume that God created the cosmos, of course, but our faith is not blind, "because the love of God has been poured out within our hearts through the Holy Spirit who was given to us."[4] In other words, we know God is real because we have met Him through Christ and are getting to know Him better and better as life goes on. "We look not at the things which are seen, but at the things which are not seen," said St. Paul, "for the things which are seen are temporal, but the things which are not seen are eternal."[5] And this perspective gives us a vibrant hope and sense of purpose for the future. Atheists like Sagan, on the other hand, find no hope in visible reality because they refuse to see the invisible reality that gave birth to it. As a result they are blind to the light of hope.

Hope looks past what is "real" to see something yet more real. How is this possible? When we are born again, God opens our spiritual eyes to comprehend the reality of His kingdom. Then, with the Holy Spirit to teach us—through prayer, Scripture, and wise counsel—what to look for, we can learn to see the world through God's eyes.

Anyone without Christ—from scientist to soccer mom— is blind to ultimate reality if he is blind to the kingdom of God. St. Paul said as much when he spoke to the Areopagus, a council of philosophers who were the elite of Greek society. Walking around Athens, the apostle had been vexed by the huge number of idols dotting the landscape. Fans of "diversity" when it came to religion, the Greeks looked at everything, it seemed, but saw nothing.

"The God who made the world and all things in it...made from one man every nation of mankind to live on all the face of the earth," Paul explained, "having determined their appointed times and the boundaries of their habitation, that they would seek God, if perhaps they might grope for Him and find Him, though He is not far from each one of us."[6]

God has designed human beings to seek Him, and everyone retains that urge, even the most sinful among us. Paul said people "grope for Him" in spiritual blindness and that those who "find Him" have their spiritual eyes opened. Thus comes a new awareness of God's providential rule and with it true hope for the future.

> *Hope looks past what is "real" to see something yet more real.*

One of the best examples of this truth comes from history, when Israel was under attack by Syria. After failing to pull off a series of surprise raids, the Syrian king called his advisors together in an effort to ferret out the traitor amongst them. Surely someone was tipping off the Israelites to their plans. But there was no traitor, interjected one of his servants. Instead, the prophet Elisha "tells the king of Israel the words that you speak in your bedroom."[7]

At once the Syrian ruler dispatched horsemen, chariots, and a large fighting force to Dothan, where Elisha lived. The next morning when Gehazi, the prophet's attendant, saw the vast Syrian army surrounding the city, he panicked. "Do not fear," Elisha said reassuringly. "For those who are with us are more than those who are with them."

Gehazi must have stood there puzzled, since he could plainly see thousands of enemy soldiers surrounding the two of them. Then Elisha prayed a simple yet powerful one-line prayer. "O LORD, I pray, open his eyes that he may see." Suddenly, the young man could see a vast, invisible contingent of angels—"horses and chariots of fire"—who had surrounded his master and him. They weren't imperiled in the least. Elisha's servant caught a glimpse into an invisible dimension that was every bit as real as the Syrian army. The Lord of hosts has always maintained a mighty troop of spiritual messengers and warriors to do His bidding. Today they continue their various missions of intervening on behalf of God's people, just as they did in Elisha's day.

You can't see them, but God's angels are surrounding you right now, even while you're reading. And when you put this book down to drive to work or to go to sleep, they will still be on the job, watching and protecting you, even working *with* you in ways you normally never notice.[8]

Were it not for the massive amount of disinformation being propagated in today's American culture war, these facts about angels might amount to a mere curiosity. But if you read the newspaper, watch television, browse the Internet, or attend a secular school, then truth is under siege at *your* house. And that makes this information very important. For without it you are blind. You are blind to the real truth, God's truth—blind to reality.

TWELVE, TEN, AND TWO

You are ultimately responsible for what you see. If you feed on the discouragement that comes with your cable TV subscription, then your hopes will eventually flag and your heart sicken. The key word here is *feed*. Watching the news every night but reading or hearing God's Word only occasionally doesn't constitute balanced intake for your eyes, ears, and mind. Discouragement will become your mind-set; you won't remain neutral. That is why the Amplified Bible says to "be careful what you are hearing. The measure [of thought and study] you give [to the truth you hear] will be the measure [of virtue and knowledge] that comes back to you—and more [besides] will be given to you who hear. For to him who has will more be given; and from him who has nothing, even what he has will be taken away [by force]."[9]

On the opposite extreme are misguided Christians who decide never to watch the news or read the paper. "I just stay in the Word," they say. But, outside the monastery walls, such an approach is wrongheaded. Reading the Bible without also tuning in to the world around you is like being a surgeon living in isolation. What use is your skill? The answer isn't to quit looking at the world around you but to submit what you see to what God's Word says. In other words, let spiritual truth serve as your foundation for reality. Remember, the spiritual realm doesn't contradict the physical; it *supersedes* it. Take, for example, the spies whom Moses sent into the Promised Land.[10]

After four hundred years of slavery—and unfulfilled promises of redemption—God had finally "shown up" to deliver the Israelites from Egypt. Can you imagine after four centuries of "hope deferred"[11] the way new hope must have blossomed in those three million hearts as they saw the hand of Almighty God at work for them? He wrought great miracles, visiting plagues upon their oppressors, folding back the sea to give them a walkway to freedom, and drowning mighty Pharaoh's army.

Now, after two years in the desert, they were camped at Kadesh-Barnea, just forty miles from the border of Canaan, the Promised Land. They were almost there! Moses had dispatched a dozen men to sneak through the perimeter, spy out the land, and bring him a report. When the twelve returned, they were toting a cluster of grapes from Eshcol that was so big it had to be suspended from a pole between their shoulders. It really was a land of milk and honey, just as God had promised!

But the fruit wasn't the only big thing about Canaan, reported ten of the spies. "There we saw the giants," they whine, "and we were like grasshoppers in our own sight, and so we were in their sight."[12] Sounds just like the bad news on television, doesn't it? Of course, Moses had sent twelve men, not just ten, and he still needed to hear from the remaining two, Joshua and Caleb. They painted a completely different picture.

> *The spiritual realm doesn't contradict the physical; it supersedes it.*

"The land which we passed through to spy out is an exceedingly good land," they reported. "If the LORD is pleased with us, then He will bring us into this land and give it to us—a land which flows with milk and honey. Only do not rebel against the LORD; and do not fear the people of the land, for they will be our prey. Their protection has been removed from them, and the LORD is with us; do not fear them."[13]

Did these two spy out a different land? "Forget this grasshopper talk," they were saying. "We'll have those giants for lunch!" The truth is, while they made the same trip as all the others, Joshua and Caleb saw something the other ten men missed. Like Moses,[14] they saw God, who was incomparably larger than any giant. The real headline that day should have read: *Twelve saw giants. Ten saw grasshoppers. Two saw God!*

That phrase "in our own sight" betrayed the truth about the ten spies. Although they were no longer living in Egypt, Egypt was living in them. They didn't see God at work in their situation any more than Pharaoh had. They chose to see themselves in terms of what the world showed them rather than in the light of God's Word. The sad thing is, the vast majority of the Israelites decided they would rather go back to Egypt than take the land. But God, exhibiting a bit of tough love, had brought them to a point of no return, and their only options were to fight for the Promised Land or to die in the desert. Sadly, they failed to make the right choice. A generation later, their children would enter the land without them, led by the only two senior citizens in the entire population—Joshua and Caleb—whose faith in God and unrelenting hope in His promises took them all the way home.

Bad News, Good News

These days, incredible pressure is being exerted on you by a media juggernaut that insists on secularizing every aspect of life.[15] It tries to control both what you see and how you interpret it, filtering everything through the lens of political correctness. Complicating the situation is the fact that you live in the age of jihad. Your nation and your way of life are under attack by militant Islam. Western media are too secularist to admit that it is a theologically motivated war, so they either twist the facts or ignore them altogether, as with Georges Sada's knowledge of Saddam Hussein's weapons of mass destruction.

Jesus said, "Do you not say, 'There are yet four months, and then comes the harvest'? Behold, I say to you, lift up your eyes and look on the fields, that they are white for harvest" (John 4:35). A spiritual harvest was all around the Lord and His disciples, but it had to be seen through spiritual eyes. They weren't used to looking at the world in that way.

If you are willing to lift up your spiritual eyes, you will see that this is the most exciting time in history to be a follower of

Jesus. For example, it took from the time of Adam to the year 1827 for the world's population to reach a billion. But during the next century 500 hundred percent, until today there are 6.4 billion people living on planet Earth, and *more than 2.1 billion of them claim to be Christian.*[16]

In his book *The Church Is Bigger Than You Think*, Patrick Johnstone suggested that during the twentieth century there was a global move of the Holy Spirit to which most Western Christians were oblivious. In the 1960s, he claims, the Spirit of the Lord swept Africa. Only 2 percent of Africans were Christians in the year 1900, yet today that continent is approximately 50 percent Christian. "Never before in history has a whole continent seen such a radical change...in a single century," says Johnstone.[17]

Johnstone says that in the 1970s the Holy Spirit expanded His harvest to South America. Whereas in 1900 there were probably no more than two hundred fifty thousand evangelical Christians in all of South America, today that number has grown to nearly sixty million. In Brazil alone, according to researcher Johnstone, there are more believers than in all of Europe combined.

Where did the Spirit move in the 1980s? "He went to Southeast Asia," says the researcher. And, in fact, at the end of the 1990s, seven of the ten largest evangelical congregations in the world were in one city: Seoul, Korea. (And the Christians there are ready to evangelize their beleaguered North Korean kinsmen when that door swings open.)

Most readers will remember how, in the 1990s, God's Spirit began to blow like a whirlwind through the communist world, across nations like Russia (where I worked extensively) and China. Some missiologists assert that there were as many as twenty-five thousand Chinese becoming Christians every day in the 1990s. Today, they claim, the church in China outnumbers—in terms of born-again believers—the church in America. In fact, as I write, the Chinese government has recently discovered that their bureau responsible for keeping track of such statistics has been grossly underestimating the growth rate of the underground church in China for fear of losing their jobs. Needless to say, that fear has been realized.

> *The Lord of hosts is planning to do something in the heart of Islam that is bigger than any of us could ever have dreamed.*

Africa in the 1960s...South America in the 1970s...Southeast Asia in the 1980s...communist bloc nations in the 1990s... The obvious question now is: Where is the wind of the Spirit blowing at the dawn of a new millennium?

I think the answer was given to us on September 11, 2001. Despite the massive tragedy and loss of life, I believe that when enraged Muslims took center stage on TV screens around the world, *we were looking at our next field of harvest.* I believe the Lord of hosts is planning to do something in the heart of Islam that is bigger than any of us could ever have dreamed. Remember: there are 1.57 billion Muslims on Planet Earth,[18] and God has a plan for them. There is a harvest coming. Be ready, and do not fear Islam. *Here and now, Jesus rules in the midst of His enemies.*[19]

I believe the wind of God's Holy Spirit will soon sweep across the Islamic world in an unprecedented way. It is blowing even now in places like the city of Erbil, in the Kurdistan region of northern Iraq, where our ministry, World Compassion, has been heavily involved for several years. I first traveled to Erbil just after the American military liberated Iraq in 2003, where we had helped to sponsor a conference of

Middle Eastern Christians. I was encouraged by the fact that fifty brave souls had attended. Not many Muslim followers of Jesus were willing to publicly acknowledge their faith in those early days of freedom.

The gathering may have been small, but it was a remarkable one, as Chaldeans, Armenians, Iranians, Assyrians, Kurds, and Arabs deeply repented to one another for their various tribal histories of blood feuds and massacres. When I returned a year later to speak to the Christian community in Erbil, their numbers had grown to two hundred fifty, with nearly all the new believers being Muslim converts. By early 2006, there were eight hundred believers in what now constituted a true church.

A few weeks later, a high-ranking Iraqi official made a public statement favoring Christian conversion over Islamic radicalism, and all heaven seemed to break loose. Hundreds more Muslims were emboldened to confess faith in Christ, and within three months, the church in the Kurdish region doubled in size to sixteen hundred fifty publicly baptized followers of Jesus, becoming perhaps the largest congregation of ex-Muslim believers in fourteen hundred years of Islamic domination.

As I write, I have just returned from the Kurdish capital yet again, having held our annual pastors seminar for a hundred leaders, the bulk of whom have become Christians within the past three years. More than three thousand baptized believers now regularly worship Jesus throughout the region. It is likely that more than double this number have committed their lives to Christ but have hesitated to submit themselves to public baptism, since for most Muslims that is an automatic death sentence, often at the hands of their own families.

Let me emphasize the point: A congregation of three thousand here in America is not news. I can point to several in my hometown of Tulsa, Oklahoma, alone. But there has not been such a large congregation of ex-Muslims in *that* region of the world since Islam began its ascendancy in the early 600s. Now, the church building they erected so recently is only large enough to hold their leadership and families. I believe that not only will their success continue, but also that their efforts are the beginning of a movement that will, like the early church, soon be accused of turning their world upside down.[20]

> *More than three thousand baptized believers now regularly worship Jesus throughout the region.*

WHAT DO YOU SEE?

If hope is going to thrive in our hearts, then we have to lift up our eyes and look for the good news in the world. There's plenty of it out there, but it is presently going unreported. Today's media, even if they were honest and objective, would still primarily give a bad report, because that is the nature of news. It isn't news when a community is peaceful, when men love their wives, well-nurtured children respect their parents, and banks prosper. No, the function of the news is to let us know when things go wrong, when murders are committed and banks are robbed.

God made us for something better than watching bad news. Yes, Christians should stay informed, but we weren't created to be news "junkies." Instead, we are instructed to put on the mind of Christ[21] and to dwell on "whatever is true, whatever is honorable, whatever is right, whatever is pure, whatever is lovely, whatever is of good repute, if there is any excellence and if anything worthy of praise."[22]

Thanks to computers and the power of the Internet, the real good news isn't that hard to find, although most news sources either ignore it or "spin" it. For example, over the past several years you've probably heard that Islam is the world's fastest-growing religion. But that's because most news outlets view religion in cultural terms, meaning that they fail to differentiate between birth rates and actual conversion rates. Hence, Islam and Hinduism (along with other Indian sects like Bahai, Jainism, and Sikhism) are all "growing" very quickly. Also, in the case of Islam, one must take into account the fact that leaving the "faith" is punishable by death.

Measure the spread of religions by actual conversion rates, however, and you'll find that the one growing fastest is Pentecostal Christianity![23] In fact, one of the most amazing testimonies of such growth comes from Iran, where various sources report the conversion of nearly one million Iranians since the dawn of the twenty-first century! This explosion of faith in Christ is due in no small part to the satellite television ministry of an Iranian-born Oklahoma pastor named Reza Safa,[24] whose broadcasts on the TBN Nejat TV Network are highly popular on Iranian television, despite the fact that it is against the law to watch them.

The mainstream news outlets would have you think of Iran as being under the thumbs of ayatollahs and political madmen. But the truth, according to Daniel, King David, and the apostle Paul, is that Jesus "rules in the kingdom of men,"[25] rules in the midst of His enemies,[26] and "must reign until He has put all His enemies under His feet."[27] Let me ask you one final time: *What do you see when you look at the world around you?* If you're looking through the eyes of hope, you will see creation much the same way as the Hubble Space Telescope sees it: without Earth's distorting atmosphere. And you will see that history, as the saying goes, really is *His* story.

ENDURING HOPE

We give thanks to God always for all of you...bearing in mind your work of faith and labor of love and steadfastness of hope in our Lord Jesus Christ.[1]

—St. Paul

ISTORY WILL SHOW that it was not only Boris Yeltsin who finally put the Soviet Union's communist government out of its misery in 1991 but also the babushkas, the little Russian grannies who took to the streets and bravely coaxed the soldiers out of their army tanks with T-shirts and cigarettes.

Babushkas look a bit like the souvenir stacking dolls that caricature them. They are typically squat and wrapped in several layers of skirts, blouses, and sweaters, their weathered faces *always* tightly framed by head scarves that crown a collision of stripes, checks, dots, and what not in faded but conflicting colors, all of it based on availability rather than style. A fixture on park benches in every town and village, they are unfailingly feisty and opinionated, whether shooing away errant skateboarders or staring down tank commanders.

In fact, it was the stinging rebuke of a babushka that changed my life and ministry.

In late 1992 Russia was entering her second year of freedom after seven decades of communism and centuries of oppression by various czars and other strongmen. Liberty, when it has existed there, has generally been short-lived, and I knew we needed to seize the day. To that end, I had begun distributing millions of Bibles across the nation.

That November, my assistant Joel and I were in Maloyaroslavets, a town of thirty thousand inhabitants about two hours southwest of Moscow. It was a typical Russian winter day, well below freezing, but we were happy to be out on the streets, engaged in something I had yearned to do for years: handing out Bibles in public.

At one point a delivery truck pulled over and parked just down the block. Then the driver raised his rear-sliding hatch and began distributing something to a rapidly forming line. But after a mere ten minutes, the man abruptly stopped, climbed back behind the wheel, and drove off, leaving dozens of people empty-handed.

"What was that about?" I asked the Russian pastor who had arranged our mission.

"It was the bread truck," he explained. "But now they're all complaining, because he only brought enough for a few people."

Just then a grumbling babushka walked over to us and asked what we were giving away. "Bibles," replied the pastor with a note of gladness. "These men have come from America to give us God's Word."

The old lady turned and glared at us, then spat out a single guttural phrase and, with a dismissive wave, turned and walked away.

"What did she say?" I asked the pastor, who looked as if

he'd just been slapped. He smiled weakly and tried to wave it off as nothing, but I insisted.

"What did she say?"

He looked downcast and was silent for a moment. Finally he translated the hobbled little woman's words. "She said... 'We can't eat your Bibles.'"

In an instant I was cut to the heart. I knew the Lord had said that man shall not live by bread alone, but I had lost sight of the fact that man cannot live *without* bread either. And even though the worst deprivation Russians had suffered under communism was the systematic denial of God's Word, the sad old grandmother was right: she couldn't eat our Bibles.

Two minutes earlier I had been serving God in the former Soviet Union... or so I thought. Now I was suddenly facing my biggest crisis of conscience in twenty-five years of ministry. How could I have been so shortsighted? If the apostle James was right that we show our faith *by* our works,[2] then my puny efforts betrayed a very one-dimensional faith for Russia. And I realized, standing there shivering in the cold, that I'd better do something about it. We needed to revamp our entire approach to missions.

> *Finally he translated the hobbled little woman's words: "We can't eat your Bibles."*

Before the year was out, Terry Law Ministries had taken the additional name World Compassion. From now on we would feed, clothe, and treat people, and *then* give them the good news of salvation for their souls as well. In the years since we have found our greatest opportunities in the world's trouble spots, places like the refugee camps of Afghanistan, the war zones of Iraq, post-tsunami Indonesia, and more recently, cyclone-ravaged Myanmar. And we have discovered that a full belly, a warm blanket, or much-needed medicine really does open people's hearts to receive the true bread of God's Word.

First Thessalonians 1:3 refers to the Christian's "work of faith and labor of love and steadfastness of hope in our Lord Jesus Christ." In this book we are primarily concerned with hope, of course, but we dare not view it in isolation; we also need to look at hope's connection with faith and love. In chapter 2 we briefly contrasted hope with faith. Now we're going to take a further look at both, as well as the "greatest" of the virtues, the one that empowers and completes this heavenly triumvirate: love.

Simply stated, *faith works, love labors, and hope endures.*

> *I knew the Lord had said that man shall not live by bread alone, but I had lost sight of the fact that man cannot live without bread either.*

FAITH WORKS

More than an adjustment in strategy, the incident in Maloyaroslavets triggered a paradigm shift in my understanding of faith. Eventually I came to see that my faith for Russia's future, although real, was unfocused and indiscriminate. Certainly I had deep affection for the peoples of the now-splintered USSR, but my "love" for them was impractical and emotional, like that of a young husband who is quick to bring his bride flowers and candy but never thinks of planning for her future. I had fallen into the very trap St. James warned about: "[If] one of you says to them, 'Go in peace, be warmed and be filled,' and yet you do not give them what is necessary for their body, what use is that?"[3]

The Lord's brother is most famous for reminding us that while faith is the *basis* for our salvation, our works are the *evidence* of it. In other words, the issue is not faith *versus* works but the simple fact that faith *works*! It's the same point Jesus made when He cursed the fig tree.[4] Faith without works is like a fig tree without figs. It might have the appearance—even the DNA—of a fig tree, but if it doesn't grow any figs, then practically speaking it is pointless to call it a *fig* tree. Faith works not to earn God's favor but *because* of God's favor. It is fruitful, focused, and purposeful. By the time Joel and I left Maloyaroslavets for Belarus three days later, the light of that truth was beginning to shine in my heart.

We went to the Children's Cancer Hospital in Minsk to see for ourselves the "children of Chernobyl," kids who had been born with birth defects because of fallout from the infamous Soviet nuclear accident two hundred miles to the south. Six years earlier, on April 26, 1986, the radioactive cloud from ground zero had passed directly over Belarus, poisoning the region's soil and food supply. In fact, 70 percent of all the radioactive particles released in the accident had fallen onto an area now known as the "exclusion zone."[5] Even today it remains the most contaminated place on earth.

Many Belarusian children born in the ensuing years had died, either from fatal birth defects or because their mothers, knowing their own breast milk was radioactive, chose to let them starve. About six hundred thousand were in various stages of precancer. The young ones in this hospital had survived thus far. To this day I cannot adequately describe their plight, except to say that when I looked into their eyes, a depth of love and compassion seized me such as I had never known. I asked the doctors what they needed most, expecting to hear that the children might appreciate toys, clothing, or something else that would bring them emotional comfort. Most Soviet-era hospitals had been places to get sicker, not better, but since Belarus was now free, I assumed that the children were receiving adequate treatment. I was wrong.

"We need transfusion machines," said the administrator, a Muslim man. "Most of these children are dying of leukemia. If we could transfuse the parent's blood into the child, we could save 50 percent of them."

Unlike the Russian Bible distribution, which had been a well-intentioned project, the health of these kids became my passion. Seeing them evoked love and compassion in me, and that gave purpose to my faith. *When faith is empowered by love, our projects become our passions.*

As soon as Joel and I arrived back in America, we obtained several blood transfusion machines. I also called the Gerber Corporation in Michigan and purchased sixty tons of food for the kids. Once the transfusion equipment had joined the massive contents of Gerber's three tractor-trailers in cargo containers at the docks in Elizabeth, New Jersey, I flew there to make sure for myself that the shipment sailed as planned. Shortly after I walked into the warehouse, I was surprised when a well-dressed gentleman strode over and introduced himself as Belarus's ambassador to the United Nations. "Why," he wanted to know, "would Americans care about Belarusian children?"

I happened to be carrying a Bible with me, so I opened it to Matthew, where Jesus said, "I was hungry, and you gave Me something to eat; I was thirsty, and you gave Me something to drink; I was a stranger, and you invited Me in; naked, and you clothed Me; I was sick, and you visited Me; I was in prison, and you came to Me."[6] The ambassador's eyes moistened as

I explained that Jesus loved those children and that we were only doing what we knew He wanted us to do.

A few weeks later I flew back to Belarus to make sure that the delivery had taken place as planned and then traveled on to neighboring Russia to meet Prime Minister Boris Yeltsin in Moscow. I arrived at the Russian White House only to learn that our meeting had been canceled at the last moment because Mr. Yeltsin had been called to London by his British counterpart John Major. Disappointed at coming all that way for nothing, I was preparing to leave when Yeltsin's press secretary invited me into his office. He closed the door behind us and came straight to the point.

"We heard about the food and transfusion equipment you sent into Belarus," he began. "Tell me, why would you Americans care about Belarusian children?"

I had no idea the Russian government had heard about our food delivery, and for a moment I stood there flustered at hearing the same question I had been asked in New Jersey. Then I took out my Bible and once again opened to Matthew chapter 25, telling this Russian official the same thing I had told the Belarusian ambassador. Jesus loved those children, and we simply had to help.

> *When faith is empowered by love, our projects become our passions.*

"Would you be willing to tell that to the Russian people?" he asked, piquing my curiosity.

"Certainly, but how would I do that?" I replied.

"On national television tonight," he answered with a tone of authority that told me he could make it happen.

That evening I found myself on a popular television program called *Good Evening, Moscow*, explaining yet again why we had purchased, shipped, and personally delivered sixty tons of food to the children in Minsk. As I talked, I noticed that my host had picked up my Bible and was gently rubbing the soft leather cover over and over, as though it were a sacred relic, like the icons so many Russians prize. Eventually, he looked down at the book and asked me what it said. I replied (shamelessly dangling a carrot) that among other words it contained Jesus's statement that "you must be born again."

"What does that mean?" he asked, taking the bait.

"I can't believe he just asked an evangelist that question on national television," I chuckled inwardly, and then turned to the cameras to explain the gospel. I knew the potential viewing audience of *Good Evening, Moscow* was about two hundred million people, spanning not only Russia but also a few border countries as well. So I went for broke and took the liberty of inviting viewers to surrender to the lordship of Jesus. After the broadcast, the producers invited me to appear on the program again the next time I was in Moscow.

I flew back to America, amazed at how unreservedly people had opened their hearts to the words of Christ once they had seen the deeds of Christ. And I understood a little better what Paul had meant when he told the Galatian Christians that faith works *through love*.[7]

LOVE LABORS

The same apostle exhorted another Greek church to "be sober, having put on the breastplate of faith and love, and as a helmet, the hope of salvation."[8] The breastplate is a shield protecting the heart, and the fact that faith and love form a single shield reveals their profound partnership.

Faith is an extension of love in the same sense that the hand is an extension of the body. Faith serves love's purposes. That is why the Bible says love is even greater than faith and hope.[9] In fact, love is so overarching that God uses it as a one-word description of Himself.[10]

Theologians sometimes forget this because they are overwhelmed by the Lord's other attributes, such as omnipotence or sovereignty. This is a big mistake, because seeing God first of all as a sovereign Ruler rather than a loving Father often makes the learned starchy and nearly everyone else fatalistic. They've seen Him as Creator in Genesis chapter 1 but not in the light of John chapter 1: "In the beginning was the Word, and the Word was with God, and the Word was God.... And the Word became flesh, and dwelt among us, and we saw His glory, glory as of *the only begotten from the Father*, full of grace and truth."[11]

> *My vision for Russia had lacked love's sensitivity and hope's focus.*

The Bible's very first words, "In the beginning," reveal a Father at work. God wasn't merely making the world to demonstrate His might and power but to give it to His Son. Far more than an awesome display of power, this was extravagant love in action, a love so great, relatively speaking, as to subsume all of His other qualities. In fact, the only other attribute that describes our great God in a single word is the one that overwhelms the mighty angels surrounding His throne: *holy.* These creatures, called *seraphim*, are surely loved by God as part of His creation,[12] but they have never known Him as their Father.[13]

We, however, are not angels; we are sons and daughters. And just as the angels are overcome by God's holiness, *we His children should be utterly smitten by His love*. It is that love coming to us that generates love coming from us. That is why Paul paired faith and love together in 1 Thessalonians 1:3, referring to that Greek congregation's "work of faith," then resorting to a more intense descriptor for love: *labor*.

The English words *work* and *labor* are sometimes used as synonyms, but any mother can tell you that labor is greater by degrees. Work, for example, may suggest mechanistic effort, but labor involves subjecting oneself to pain. (A machine works, but it does not labor.) Like a mother laboring in birth pangs, love is not preoccupied with its own feelings but with its object. The reason I could help those ravaged children in Minsk, Belarus, was because God's love compelled me to forget myself and think practically on their behalf.

My mistake in Maloyaroslavets, on the other hand, had been due to fulfilling my own dream of serving God rather than being sensitive to the people's need for bread. *My vision for Russia had lacked love's sensitivity and hope's focus.*

HOPE ENDURES

Have you ever seen a black-and-white drawing that is actually two pictures in one? Probably the best known is the one that depicts a young Victorian lady when you focus on the black ink, and an old hag when you stare at the white space. What you see depends upon your point of view. In much the same way, the writer of the New Testament letter to the Hebrews also combines two pictures in his portrayal of hope. First, there's the scene of a criminal, fleeing to something called a "city of refuge."

> God desired [that]...we who have fled for refuge might have strong encouragement *to hold fast to the hope set before us. We have this as a sure and stead-*

fast anchor of the soul, a hope that enters into the
inner place behind the curtain, where Jesus has gone
as a forerunner on our behalf, having become a high
priest forever after the order of Melchizedek.[14]

In ancient Israel, if a man accidentally killed someone and
was being pursued, he could flee to one of six cities of refuge,
run to the local house of God, and grab the horns of the large
brass altar where the priests offered sacrifices. As long as the
manslayer clung to those horns, he was safe and assured of a
proper trial. So, the first image in our dual portrait strongly
encourages sinners—you and me, whose sins killed the Son
of God—to cling to our hope in Christ, because it is the only
chance we have of escaping the guilt that pursues us.

Having set this first scene, the "artist" of Hebrews super-
imposes it onto a second one with a nautical theme. Now the
horns of the altar to which we cling become an anchor, set
behind a curtain through which only a high priest can pass.
The Jewish readers of this chapter would have instantly recognized this second altar as the ark of the covenant, which sat in
the holy of holies, the place where once a year the high priest
would apply blood to the mercy seat to atone for the nation's
sins. Bible commentator Louis Talbot explains the nautical
metaphor quite well.

The Greek harbors were often cut off from the sea by
sandbars over which the larger ships dared not pass
till the full time came in. Therefore, a lighter vessel, a
"forerunner," took the anchor and dropped it in the
harbor. From that moment the ship was safe from the
storm, although it had to wait for the tide, before it
could enter the harbor....The entrance of the small
vessel into the harbor, the forerunner carrying the

ship's anchor, was the pledge that the ship would safely enter the harbor when the tide was full. And because Christ, our "forerunner," has entered heaven itself, having torn asunder everything that separates the redeemed sinner from the very presence of God, He Himself is the Pledge that we, too, shall one day enter the harbor of our souls and the very presence of God, in the New Jerusalem.[15]

Are you beginning to see the incredible nature of your hope in Christ? You were a manslayer whose sins killed the Lamb of God, so you fled to a place of refuge in God's house, where you now cling to your only hope of survival. Yet Jesus has taken that horned altar and turned it into an anchor of hope. Moreover, He has become your "forerunner," the one person able to successfully navigate His way into the presence of God for you. And He has become your high priest, atoning for your sins once for all time by His own blood, firmly anchoring your hopes to Himself.

> *You can endure the strongest of storms because you have something better than a ticket to heaven; you have an anchor called hope and a forerunner named Jesus.*

The ocean is the most unstable surface on earth; it is always moving. That is why every boat, large or small, must have an anchor. Your own ship of life might be rocking and rolling on a sea of rough circumstances so severe that you've begun to think there is no hope for you. But "We have an anchor that keeps the soul / Steadfast and sure while the billows roll,"[16] says an old hymn from my childhood. And what is that anchor? It's your hope. That's why you must strengthen that vital cord at all costs, so that just as Christ cannot be moved, neither can you.

Do you remember what I said about different points of view? Well, when it comes to your circumstances, there are two perspectives worth seeing. From your vantage point, Jesus is making a way for you into God's presence. And from God's point of view, Jesus's arrival in the throne room two thousand years ago was a sure sign that you were on your way!

Years ago, my buddy Dennis Bjorgan and I spent twenty-eight days aboard a Norwegian freighter. We were determined to make it to our very first missionary destination of South Africa, and that old boat, loaded with timber, offered the only ticket we could afford. So we packed up our gear in western Canada and headed to Montreal, where our "cruise ship" was anchored. Having grown up on the dusty prairies of western Canada, I was excited when we climbed aboard that freighter. Never mind that our quarters consisted of a windowless eight-by-eight cubicle with a ceiling just inches above our heads and bunks attached to the wall. We were voyagers now—Africa, here we come!

A few hours later, as we steamed down the Gulf of St. Lawrence toward the Atlantic Ocean, our sailing fantasies were abruptly cut short. Colliding undersea currents called "rollers" began tossing our little vessel to and fro and up and down like a chef salad. Dennis and I hung on for dear life, hoping it wouldn't last long. But the rollers were only an appetizer for the main course awaiting us in the middle of the Atlantic: two full-blown storms with waves taller than our ship that flung us around our little square room like dice in a box. Believe me, dropping anchor in Capetown, South Africa, and crawling ashore seemed every bit as sweet as going to heaven. (And I have chosen to fly that route ever since.)

Life might seem unbearably rough for you right now, but

I want to assure you that nothing in the world can stop you from making it to your destination in God. You can endure the strongest of storms because you have something better than a ticket to heaven; you have an anchor called hope and a forerunner named Jesus. He has already set your destination and established your route. He wants you to be strongly encouraged to "take hold of the hope set before" *you*,[17] because the forerunner is pulling you home.

ABOUNDING HOPE

Hope is the thing with feathers
That perches in the soul,
And sings the tune—without the words,
And never stops at all.[1]

—EMILY DICKENSON
"HOPE IS THE THING WITH FEATHERS"

"WHAT ARE YOU going to do now?" Oral Roberts asked me, his eyes fixed in a penetrating gaze.

The president of ORU had heard I was back on campus and had called me to his spacious office atop the diamond-shaped Learning Resource Center. Sitting there in the huge glass suite with its panoramic view, I felt small and more than a little dumbfounded. I had just given him a glowing report about Living Sound's first year of ministry in South Africa.

We had sung and preached well over four hundred times in ten months in schools, churches, stadiums, open fields, and concert halls, setting attendance records in several venues. We had also broken through the racial barriers of apartheid,[2] ministering not only to separate black and white audiences but also to integrated crowds as well. Best of all, we had seen nearly seven thousand people come to Christ, most of them school-aged.

President Roberts had given one or two slight nods while I waxed eloquent, yet he seemed almost disinterested. He wanted me to look to the *future*, but I had been too busy celebrating the present to start planning for anything new.

"Terry, the greatest danger that can happen to a man of God is the danger of security," he said, pointing his index finger at me. "Over the years I've seen so many ministers build a comfortable nest for their ministry and church and family. But that can be the curse that destroys your call and prevents the will of God from being accomplished in your life. I want you to dare to dream something so big that God has to intervene and save you in order for the thing to be successful."

That long finger still had me in its crosshairs, and I wasn't about to move.

"I want you to live on the cutting edge of insecurity for the rest of your life. If you do, then you'll always live on the cutting edge of faith as well."

Four decades of experience have proven the late visionary right. I was insecure about our first trip behind the iron curtain in 1972, especially when we arrived in Poland only to find out our invitation had come from the Youth Communist Party, who thought we were a secular rock group. I was nervous when I stepped onstage in their nightclub that evening and shocked everyone (including myself) by proclaiming Marx and Lenin wrong and Jesus as the only way to life. I was even more nervous when the local party leaders whisked me into the basement for questioning. But with the evening's fireworks came instant fame throughout that nation.

I was insecure two years later, when a priest invited the team to sing at his Roman Catholic Church in Tampa, Florida. After all, we were Protestants, just like God Himself! What would we sing or say to a crowd I didn't even think knew Jesus? But the remarkable engagement that followed would lead us back to Poland, this time into the nation's Catholic churches and to the home of Poland's junior cardinal, Karol Wojtyla, whom the world would later come to know as Pope John Paul II.

I was still getting my sea legs in 1980 when sixty thousand people came to St. Peter's Square for our Vatican concert, where the Polish pontiff tapped his toe to our music, his personal copy of our latest album cradled under his arm. Then he bestowed an apostolic blessing that in years to come would take us into Roman Catholic cathedrals and churches all over the world. In country after country, the Catholic faithful would line up, sometimes hundreds deep, for the laying on of hands for healing and salvation.

> *"I want you to live on the cutting edge of insecurity for the rest of your life. If you do, then you'll always live on the cutting edge of faith as well."*

Was I insecure? Definitely. Was there danger in it? Absolutely. But if I hadn't been willing to accept the insecurity, I would never have developed the faith to fulfill God's plan for my ministry. Nor would I have developed the tremendous sense of hope that now causes my heart to leap when a new opportunity arises. In fact, I can truthfully say I've come to a place, as St. Paul described it, of *abounding* hope.

Now may the God of hope fill you with all joy and peace in believing, so that you will abound in hope by the power of the Holy Spirit.[3]

ABOUNDING HOPE

God desires to bring each of us into a life of abounding hope, hope that is strong, stable, radiant, unshakable, confident, and so plentiful that it spills over onto people around us. But in order to get us there, He takes us through His required process.[4]

- We must suffer tribulation (trouble).
- Tribulation develops perseverance.
- Perseverance develops proven character.
- Proven character develops hope.

Hope that has not gone through the crucible of suffering, perseverance, and experience is really only wishful thinking. It can't be gotten "right now" anymore than wishing for a baby can produce one on the spot. There are no shortcuts to abounding hope.

One time a lady approached a friend of mine and asked him to "pray that God will give me patience." Bob's perpetual smile never broke as he closed his eyes and laid a hand on her shoulder. "Lord, I pray that You will give this woman tribulation," he said.

"That's not what I asked for," she said, sweeping his hand away. "I asked for patience." Still smiling, he put his hand back on her shoulder and prayed once more, "Lord, give her tribulation."

Again she protested and, now frustrated, asked, "Why do you keep praying that?"

"Well, if you want patience," Bob gently explained, "there's only one way to get it: The Bible says, 'Tribulation brings about patience.'"

More than simply surviving life's trials, God wills that we abound in hope, our eyes eagerly focused on the future, not naïvely, but because we are encouraged by *His* track record in our lives. This kind of hope won't let us down.[5] In fact, the gift of God's Holy Spirit makes real hope impervious to discouragement.

WHEN, NOT IF

Rather than causing all of life's troubles to stop when we give our lives to Jesus, God allows some of them to continue, using them to strengthen our hope. These trials may come through the death of a loved one or through the simple separation of distance. They might come when a job is lost or an economic crash wipes out personal savings. Tribulation can come through common frustration or complicated depression, through humiliation, deception in business, or betrayal in a relationship. It can take the form of a hurricane, a car accident, divorce, rejection, or some apparently random tragedy, such as a child's death at the hands of a drunk driver.

> *Hope that has not gone through the crucible of suffering, perseverance, and experience is really only wishful thinking.*

St. Paul and his traveling partner, Barnabas, took the certainty of suffering a step further and called it a "must" if we want to enter the kingdom of God.[6] We must be tested, or we will never enter the kingdom, never learn to persevere, never develop real character, and never abound in hope. Yet this indispensable aspect of the Christian life goes unreported by many pastors who fear it would shrivel church attendance.

New Christians especially need to know about the certainty of tribulation. We tell them that God wants to heal and prosper them and that they're going to heaven. But if we don't incorporate the "must" of suffering, we're just selling them a bed of roses. We need to warn them that along with—or perhaps ahead of—the healing and prosperity, tribulation is on its way. Paul puts this necessary suffering in perspective by calling it "momentary, light affliction [that] is producing for us an eternal weight of glory far beyond all comparison."[7] In other words, being born again doesn't mean that all of our problems are solved but that they have been made incomparably beneficial to us. This is true even when it seems our hopes have died. As David Augsburger explains, the apparent death of hope may actually be its birth.

> Hope is kindled by both success and failure, by pleasure and pain, by calm and crisis. It is nourished by constant support; it is exercised and strengthened by difficulty and adversity.... [This] is necessary because strong, resilient, undiscourageable hope is created only as it is tested, tempered, transformed.[8]

TRIED BY GOLD

Real hope, like fine gold, must be purified by fire. Job was referring to this when he said, "But He knows the way I take; when He has tried me, I shall come forth as gold."[9]

Make no mistake: you will be tested, either by persecution for your faith in Christ or by success because of it. Or both.

Yet, gold can also *be* the fire of testing. Jesus once told a parable about both persecution and "the deceitfulness of wealth,"[10] and then explained Himself in detail.

When affliction or persecution arises because of the word, immediately he falls away. And the one on whom seed was sown among the thorns, this is the man who hears the word, and the worry of the world and the deceitfulness of wealth choke the word, and it becomes unfruitful.[11]

You will notice that the Savior opens His explanation with that little word *when* in referring to the inevitability of "affliction or persecution." But then He mentions the test hardly anyone braces for, even though it is just as certain as affliction. It is "the worry of the world and the deceitfulness of wealth." If the enemy of your soul cannot defeat you through outright persecution, you can be sure he'll try to turn prosperity into a curse on your life.

I once heard my friend Derek Prince make a profound comment on this parable. "In the Christian West," he observed, "for every one that falls away [from Christ] because of persecution, ten will fall away because of their worries over wealth." Make no mistake: you will be tested, either by persecution for your faith in Christ or by success because of it. Or both.

The Process: Tribulation

The road to abounding hope is a process of tribulation, perseverance, and character growth.[12] The prophet Isaiah alluded to this process with a powerful metaphor: "Even youths grow tired and weary, and young men stumble and fall; but those who hope in the LORD will renew their strength. They will soar on wings like eagles; they will run and not grow weary, they will walk and not be faint."[13]

We all know how majestically eagles soar through the heavens, but how do they manage to get up there in the first place? I always pictured them mounting up with lots of flapping, but the truth is, eagles hardly ever flap. Instead, they merely extend their disproportionately long wings and negotiate wind currents called "thermals." Twisting and twirling, they constantly adjust their bodies, turning opposing winds into friendly ones. In fact, wind and storms, rather than keeping eagles on the ground, actually enable them to soar that much higher.

When I saw this passage I knew I had to learn more, so I invoked what theologians call the "law of first mention" and searched the Bible to see what eagles signified in earlier passages. I found the first reference way back in the fifth book of the Bible:

> Like an eagle that stirs up its nest, that hovers over its young, He spread His wings and caught them, He carried them on His pinions. The LORD alone guided [Israel], and there was no foreign god with him.
> —DEUTERONOMY 32:11–12

The apostle Paul told the Corinthians that Israel's experience in the wilderness was "an example…written for our instruction."[14] In other words, the way God guided the Israelites into the Promised Land is also the way He guides us into the fullness of Christ—into abounding hope.

We all think baby birds are cute, even "ugly cute" eaglets. And we don't like the idea of some poor little thing falling from its mother's nest, flapping wildly as it plummets toward the rocky earth below. But that is exactly what happens to every little eaglet that ever learns to fly. And what's more, Mama is the one who drops him.

This is God's process with us and the real reason tribulation comes. Think about it: A cute baby eagle sits in a cozy, downy nest perched thousands of feet above the earth, every meal delivered right on time. Would he *ever* willingly jump out of such luxury? Of course not! Why should he learn to fly with a deal like that? The eaglet doesn't know that he cannot live that way forever. In fact, if he's going to survive, he *must* learn to fly. He doesn't realize his nest was never meant to be permanent, and indeed, underneath all that softness his mother has built a substructure specifically designed to make him jump.

Several weeks earlier, when the mother eagle first sensed she was about to hatch some eggs, she started gathering large branches from the earth below, and much like a carpenter, she assembled a scaffold. Then she scoured the field and forest for sharp sticks, briars, and thorns and proceeded to coat the inside of that scaffold with a layer of all things prickly. Finally she made a third layer, the one her eaglets would like. She covered all the sharp spots with fern and moss, maybe even a rabbit's skin, and then topped the whole thing off with soft downy feathers plucked from her own breast. Her babies—let's call them Jack and Jill—can thus recline in total comfort in the familiar feel and smell of their mother.

Once hatched, Jack and Jill revel in the lap of luxury as Mama brings them delicacies like fish and mice. All they have to do is sit there in the nest and open their beaks while she drops in the food. Life is wonderful, just like it probably was during your early days as a Christian. You prayed; God answered. You got sick; He healed you. He took care of everything while you just sat there with your mouth wide open, waiting for more. He even seemed to overlook a few bad habits...for a while. But since God made both eagles and people to fly, He has designed a process both have to go through. Look back at Deuteronomy 32:11. It says the mother eagle "stirs up its nest." What does that mean? In a word: trouble.

One day Mama returns from her hunting trip, and she

doesn't have anything in her mouth. Jack and Jill, hungry at the sight of her, are bewildered. Mama has a strange look in her eye. Suddenly she rears back with her huge beak, stabs downward into the downy nest, and removes a big batch of feathers, moss, and skin. Then she hops over to the edge and drops it ten thousand feet into the valley. Turning back into the nest, she removes another big chunk of the living room and drops it, then another and another, until there's nothing left except briars and brambles and everything that makes life totally uncomfortable. At this point, Jack and Jill, if they were human, probably would blame their thorny circumstances on the devil. But Mama is fully in charge, orchestrating everything, and even though the youngsters don't realize it, *their present discomfort is for their future benefit.* If they don't learn to fly, they will die.

The Process: Perseverance

After the food stops coming, the eaglets' survival instinct kicks in, and they begin looking for a way out of their thorny predicament. From their point of view, Mama has forgotten they exist.

One day, apparently ignoring them, she sits on the edge of the nest doing absolutely nothing. Then, as a gust of warm air blows in, she spreads her enormous wings, loosens her talons from the edge of the nest, and with a blood-curdling scream, launches herself into the air, where she then simply hovers a few feet away in space. There's no need to flap. She understands thermals—warm air currents—and how to negotiate them. Able to hover here for hours, she's teaching her youngsters how to ride the wind. When Deuteronomy 32:11 says that God watches over His people as an eagle "hovers over its young," it's referring to the way He teaches us to negotiate the way of the wind of His Spirit in our lives.

Remember how Nicodemus was puzzled by Jesus's reference to being born again? "How can a man be born when he is old?" he asked. "He cannot enter a second time into his mother's womb and be born, can he?"[15] The Savior told him not to be amazed at the strange turn of a phrase. "The wind blows where it wishes and you hear the sound of it, but do not know where it comes from and where it is going; so is everyone who is born of the Spirit."[16]

When we're spiritual eaglets, we feel happy and secure. We have answered prayers, happy families, good jobs; everything's going great. But then the wind blows, and it may carry us places that we don't want to go.

Over the years I've discovered that learning to cooperate with the wind of the Spirit has resulted in my greatest productivity for the kingdom of God. Furthermore, what I usually initially perceive to be an opposing gale invariably turns out to be a ticket to high adventure—if I will *adjust my position and stick with it.* This is perseverance.

Shortly after the attacks of September 11, 2001, I was watching televised news coverage of the refugee crisis brought to Afghanistan by the Western coalition's war on the Taliban. The images of widows and orphans fleeing for their lives into barren desert camps startled me. I still remember the haunted looks on their faces and the reporters' description of their desperate situation. As I watched those sad scenes on television, I heard a voice in my heart, quoting a saying I had heard many years earlier: "Do you want to curse the darkness or light a candle?"

The thought came so suddenly that I was startled, and at once I replied with the obvious: "I'd far sooner light a candle." Then I heard it more clearly. "Everybody in America and the West is cursing the darkness of Islam, but I want you to go over there and light a candle." I had no idea what lighting a candle would mean in practical terms, but somehow I knew that if I went to Afghanistan, God would show me.

My staff was taken aback when I walked into the office the next day and told them I was going to Afghanistan. "Where in Afghanistan?" they asked, and I said I didn't know. I just knew I had to go.

A week later my associate Joel and I flew to Islamabad, Pakistan. After clearing airport customs we went outside to hail a taxi, only to be greeted by a sea of portraits of Osama bin Laden on the sides of all the cabs. Our driver explained, "Over here no one believes bin Laden blew up the World Trade Center. They believe it was done by Israeli intelligence with the help of the CIA." Probably 80 percent of the people in Central Asia believed it, he said.

> "Do you want to curse the darkness or light a candle?"

Within hours Joel and I found out we could get closer to the war by heading south, so the next day we flew to the city of Quetta on the Afghan border. We knew no one there and had no plan of action. In eagle terms, we were "winging it." We arrived at the Serena Hotel, which had become a fortress, its flat roof turned into a machine gun emplacement that guarded a makeshift TV studio for the BBC and CNN, who were broadcasting from opposite sides. I soon learned that Peter Kessler, the UN high commissioner for refugees, lived in the hotel. I went to see him the next day and told him we wanted to help refugees, especially widows and orphans.

"I'm sorry, but I can't allow that," he said, explaining that as Americans, Joel and I would be killed as soon as we entered a camp. "Besides, we've just gone into lockdown. Nobody can leave this hotel for the next week."

I prayed as I walked along the corridor back to my room. God had spoken to me to go to Afghanistan and help the refugees. Surely there had to be a way. Then I remembered that one of our ministry partners back in Tulsa, Dr. Christina Earls, had told me about her brother, David, who lived in Pakistan. Joel checked the phone number she had given us—it was a number in Quetta!

We called David, and he quickly came to the hotel. "We want to get into the refugee camps," I told him, "but we've been refused because it's too dangerous."

"I pastor a church very near the border, and there's a camp of nine thousand refugees not far from us," he replied, referring to the Killi Fazo camp that had been featured on the cover of *TIME* magazine the previous week. "I can get you in." Just like that, the impossible had become possible. The next day, Pastor David somehow got us out of the hotel lockdown, across the border, and into the camp, where we were able to minister to people's needs. Soon thereafter we were able to return with truckloads of food.

Just as critical, however, was the need for clothing and blankets, especially for the children, twelve of whom were, on average, freezing to death every night. Moreover, November's subzero weather would turn even colder by January. We had to help quickly.

We headed to a local market back in Quetta and bought every shop's entire inventory, five thousand jackets for teens and smaller children. I was angered that nobody there had cared enough to take this warm clothing the short distance to the camp. It was, relatively speaking, as easy as lighting a candle, yet two foreigners had to come from the other side of the world to do it.

I took several teams and tons of relief supplies back to those camps over the next two years. At times we were mobbed and once almost killed. But it was the grateful looks in the eyes of those precious children that overwhelmed my sense of danger and kept us going back. We also took literature and a living witness to the love of Christ, and although security prevents me from saying much, I can report that, at this writing, there's an underground church network of several hundred believers operating in and around Afghanistan's capital city of Kabul.

> *We bought every shop's entire inventory, five thousand jackets for teens and smaller children.*

How did it all begin? By sitting in a living room chair and watching the evening news just like millions of other Americans. What was the difference? I've always been hungry to follow the way of the Wind. And on that autumn night in Tulsa, I felt Him blowing.

THE PROCESS: CHARACTER

The eaglets can watch their mother ride the wind day after day, but if they're going to learn to fly, they have to leave the nest. So, one day the mother simply gathers little Jack by the scruff of his neck and drops him into the air, two miles above the valley floor. It's a wild ride on the way down, and out of sheer reflex the terrified little eaglet begins flapping his wings as hard as he can. He is hopelessly clumsy, of course, and plummeting toward certain death. But then, just before he hits the ground, Mama is suddenly beneath him. Catching the eaglet on her back, she carries him up into the heavens, then tips onto her side and drops him a second time.

This is it: graduation day. Dropping her eaglet time after time, Mama is expanding his comfort zone by repeatedly violating it. And sure enough, by evening Jack has learned to fly. His mother's perseverance has become his own. He's an eagle now.

This is how God led Israel, and it is how He leads us. He stops spoon-feeding us and stirs up our nest. We become hungry and uncomfortable, frustrated, maybe even emotionally drained. What has happened to our intimacy with God? Why has He forsaken us? Of course, Father God is still there. He's hovering overhead, out there where we don't want to look for Him, where we're afraid to follow. But that's where the wind is blowing, you see. And He's showing us that we're made in His image. We have wings—spirits—just like Him, and we have to learn to depend on them.

ON WINGS OF HOPE

Throughout my adult life, God has repeatedly dropped me into situations where I didn't think I could pull up in time. Yet in every circumstance He has either caught me (and dropped me again) or I've learned to fly. The process has made me stronger. I no longer panic in the face of trouble and find it easier to persevere when things get tough. In fact, most of what I used to define as "tough" doesn't even raise my spiritual pulse these days. That's not because the storms of life are weaker—they aren't—but because God in me is stronger. I've learned to recognize the wind of the Spirit in the storm and to ride that wind to a higher plane. It's the place of abounding hope, the place where eagles don't just soar but the place where they build their nests.

Never forget Isaiah's promise that "those who hope in the LORD will renew their strength. They will soar on wings like eagles; they will run and not grow weary, they will walk and not be faint."[17] Never forget that the road to genuine hope starts with troubles. Or to put it another way, *your troubles are a sign that there is hope for you.* Those troubles will develop your ability to persevere, and perseverance will develop and prove your character, strengthening your confidence in the goodness of God, which is *your hope.*[18]

> *Never forget that the road to genuine hope starts with troubles.*

I believe you can learn to "soar on wings like eagles, [to] run and not grow weary, [to] walk and not faint." I believe you can learn to turn your face *into* the wind of God's Spirit and fly into the life of purpose and destiny He has designed for you. I believe you can build a nest up there and *live* on the heights of hope, always ready for the wind to blow, ready for that voice in your spirit when He says, "Come on. Let's go for a ride!"

CHOOSING HOPE

Between stimulus and response there is a space. In that space lies our freedom and power to choose our response. In those choices lie our growth and our happiness.[1]
—STEPHEN COVEY

BROTHER ANDREW, THE man best known as "God's Smuggler," has no tolerance for the spirit of fatalism that has spread like a virus through much of the contemporary church, as he explained in the following account.

Some time ago I heard two Christian women discussing the plight of hostages being held by Middle Eastern terrorists.

"I feel sorry for those poor men and their families," one of the women remarked, "but really, this is God's problem, not ours. We have to remember that He has already decided how their stories are going to turn out."

The other woman sighed. "Yes," she said, "but it's frustrating! It seems we're all being held hostage by

the evil people in the world—the terrorists and dicta-
tors, the drug dealers, the criminals..."

The first woman smiled and patted her friend's
arm. "Well, that's how it looks," she said comfort-
ingly, "but we know God has His reasons for allowing
these things. Even when we don't understand those
reasons, we can be sure that nothing happens outside
His will."

As I listened, I felt indignation rising within me. I
could barely control the urge to turn to them and say,
"What's the matter with you? Why are you talking
this way? You're not helpless! God has given you the
power to change that situation! Why don't you use it?
Why don't you pray?"[2]

With whom do you identify in this story—with the two
ladies or with Brother Andrew? I know it's easy to concede,
"He's right. Of course we should pray." That's the spiritual-
sounding answer. *But what about the way you actually live
your life?* The sad truth is that most Christians don't pray very
much and usually invoke God's sovereignty as their excuse.
But why? Why don't we pray? I'll let my coauthor Jim Gilbert
answer that. As I write, he has just returned from a world
missions conference on the West Coast.

Before I got up to speak the pastor asked if anyone
needed prayer. Then he invited people standing
near those in need to walk over, touch them on
the shoulder, and pray for them. But hardly anyone
moved, and, sadly, some people stood with an
upraised hand and no one to pray for them. I knew
why and decided to confront the problem head-on as
an introduction to my message.

"Here we are, talking about going to the ends of the earth with the gospel, yet most of you didn't bother to walk ten feet to pray for your own brothers and sisters nearby," I began. "The reason, plain and simple, is that you don't really think your prayers will make a difference. You didn't step out because you think prayer—your prayer—is pointless."

It was a risky way to start, but doing anything else would have been hypocritical. How could they hope to take on the third world when they were so fatalistic about making a difference in their own?

Such fatalism about prayer has captured countless Christians who have also bought into the lie that hope amounts to nothing more than wishful thinking, that it always includes at least a shred of uncertainty. But remember what we said in chapter 1: *hope is a choice, a deliberate act rather than a spontaneous feeling*, that you must often make *in spite of* your feelings.

> *It's easy to concede, "Of course we should pray." That's the spiritual-sounding answer. But what about the way you actually live your life?*

Choice always includes alternatives: soup or salad, window or aisle, paper or plastic. You must *choose* to wear the helmet of hope. Or you can choose the mind-set of *fatalism*, which we call *resignation* in its early stages and *despair* when it is full blown. But even despair—contrary to popular opinion—is not something you fall into; it is as deliberately chosen as hope. That might sound harsh, but you must come to grips with the reality that, ultimately, you are not a victim. You may have been cheated and abused all your life, but God has given you the power to choose how you will live in response to your past. Choice is a gift that no one can take from you. You are constantly choosing, to some extent, either hope or resignation. There is no middle ground. *My prayer throughout the writing of this book has been that you will allow hope to become a reflex, your automatic response in every situation.*

As previously noted, this will require nothing less than a paradigm shift, a total transformation in your thinking, from a mind-set of habitual fatalism to one of perpetual hope. I am confident you need to make this shift simply because fatalism is so pervasive in today's society, from boardroom to classroom, at home and at church—*especially* at church. Brother Andrew calls the ecclesiastical variety by the self-contradictory term "Christian fatalism"[3] and exhorts believers to "fight it for all we are worth, because it is the most powerful weapon the enemy is using at this point in history to defeat the purposes of God."[4]

> *You are constantly choosing, to some extent, either hope or resignation. There is no middle ground.*

Andrew is right. On the one side are those who think that going to heaven is all that matters. They would curse the darkness and yet do little about it, since "it's all been prophesied." Such was the case in 1991 when hard-line Russian communists overthrew Soviet Premier Mikhail Gorbachev. Within hours, prophecy "experts" were on Christian television, explaining how such a crackdown had been inevitable because a free Russia just didn't line up with the Bible's predictions. Of course, five days later the coup collapsed, taking the whole communist system down with it.

How could Christians, whom Jesus called the light of the world,[5] become so adept at predicting darkness? And if we are inheriting the earth, why are so many of us preoccupied with leaving it? Didn't Jesus say that the singular sign of the end would be that, "This gospel of the kingdom shall be preached in the whole world as a testimony to all the nations, and *then* the end will come"?[6] To predict history's end before the gospel has been preached to all the world's peoples directly contradicts our Lord. I believe Him, and that's why I do what I do.

Fatalism's flip side is depicted by the two ladies from Brother Andrew's story. Extreme adherents of the doctrine of predestination, they sit idle as well, having been lulled into the smug reassurance that all the trouble in the world is a part of God's inscrutable plan. "Bad things can only happen if God allows them, so He must have His reasons," they coo, making their lack of concern sound like humility. Indeed, they might as well say *Insha'Allah,* the Muslim catchall phrase for "God willing."

Regarding evil, then, both sides are fatalistic and quite ill prepared to inherit the earth. And if either represents a godly attitude, then why would Jesus teach His disciples to pray, "Your will be done, on earth as it is in heaven"?[7] Would He command us to pray for something He knows cannot happen? Of course not! The fact that God's will is perfectly executed in heaven, combined with Jesus's command that we should pray for the same level of obedience to take place here on Earth, should stir incredible hope in every Christian. The good news is that Jesus told us to pray this way because it is entirely possible for God's will to be carried out on Earth. *The gospel was and is designed to succeed!*

Is God Willing?

Ending every prayer with a resigned "God willing" assumes that you can never truly know what He wants. That is false humility and is the very opposite of what Jesus actually taught. The Savior's command that we should pray *to* the Father—rather than refer to Him in the third person like Muslims—assumes a relationship with Him. *We are His agents bowing before His throne, not the earthbound victims of an uncertain fate.* "Your will be done on earth, as it is in heaven" is more a pledge than a petition. We are to pray for God's will with the confidence that He will show us how to accomplish it.

Being a joint heir with Jesus means you get to participate in His reign, which is precisely why St. Paul said, "Those who receive the abundance of grace and of the gift of righteousness will reign *in life* through the One, Jesus Christ."[8] This doesn't mean you will never face sickness again or that you can magically choose wealth without working for it. Bad things do happen to good people. I know, because I lost my wife and the mother of my three young children in a car accident that I could never be persuaded to characterize as "good" in any sense of the word. But the bottom line is that God, in giving you the power to choose, has also given you the freedom and authority to thrive rather than merely survive.

The mega-bestseller *The 7 Habits of Highly Successful People* made author Stephen Covey one of the world's most sought-after leadership consultants. As he traveled, Covey discovered what he came to call *The 8th Habit*, which he defines as your ability to "find your voice and inspire others to find theirs."[9] The key to finding your voice, he says, is to learn to exercise what he calls "birth-gifts." And the "one gift that enables all the gifts to be used" is the power to choose.[10]

Your power to choose is on display throughout the Scriptures in the form of hundreds of *conditional promises* that were "written for our instruction, so that through perseverance and the encouragement of the Scriptures we might have hope."[11] This type of promise would be meaningless without the little word *if* that He has tied to each one like a ribbon around a Christmas gift: you can't open the gift until you deal with the ribbon! For example:

- You can hear God's voice, *if* you're willing (Hebrews 3:7). But until you choose, you cannot hear.
- God will answer you and show you great things, *if* you will call to Him (Jeremiah 33:3). But until you choose, you have no voice.
- Ask whatever you wish and it will be done for you, *if* you abide in Christ and His words abide in you (John 15:7). But until you choose, you cannot be encouraged.
- God will keep you in perfect peace, *if* you trust Him and keep your mind "stayed" on Him (Isaiah 26:3, NKJV). But until you choose, you will never know peace.
- He will heal the land, *if* His people humble themselves and pray and seek His face and turn from wickedness (2 Chronicles 7:14). But until you choose, you cannot be healed.

And as they say on television, "But wait, there's more!" According to Psalm 30:11–12 and Isaiah 61:1–3, you can choose to trade your mourning for dancing, your sackcloth for gladness, your silence for a song of praise, your ashes for beauty, your sorrows for the oil of joy, your bondage for liberty, your broken heart for healing, and your spirit of heaviness for a garment of praise!

Yet, as nonsensical as it would be, you *can* turn down the offer. You can take off your helmet, ignore God's Word, and let the enemy of your soul pile on because:

- You think God is trying to teach you something.
- It's all in His plan.
- Nothing can be done about it until Jesus comes.

It's your choice.

THE MOMENT OF CHOICE

Paul Anka, among the most successful songwriters of all time, once said that the secret to writing songs is to begin. That's true of many disciplines, isn't it? Whether you're planning on keeping a diary, learning to swim, or eating right and losing weight, there's no time like the present. The same principle holds true with regard to choosing hope. If you wait to start "feeling" it or hold out for some improvement in your situation to inspire it, you'll still be waiting ten years from now. Choosing to hope means coming to grips with the fact that the time to start is now. You don't prepare for it like college. You just start, right now, in *this moment*. Stephen Covey describes the moment of choice in this way:

> Between stimulus and response there is a space. In that space lie our freedom and power to choose our response. In those choices lie our growth and our happiness.[12]

Covey goes on to explain that "it is in the *use* of that space that the opportunity to enlarge it exists."[13] Whether your response is thoughtful and deliberate or emotional and reactive, it is still the response *you choose.*

I remember my own discovery of Covey's "space." It was November 2007, and my schedule was much too busy. I had spent a week in the Middle East, then flown home to Tulsa for one meeting, before heading to Minneapolis for a large conference, and then back home again. Flying nearly twenty thousand miles in less than two weeks is difficult anytime, but I had actually begun feeling chest pains back in Dubai, near the beginning of the trip, and had forced myself to keep going.

For ten days I had blocked the pain, but now, visiting with my future wife, Barbara, it hit me with a vengeance. My solar plexus was on fire, and I couldn't get a full breath. There was only one thing to do, and that was to head for the hospital. Minutes later I was counting ceiling tiles as an emergency room attendant whisked my stretcher through the halls of South Crest Hospital to the cardiac unit and a waiting team of doctors.

> *I knew that my hope in God couldn't change my diagnosis, but it could certainly change my response.*

"Mr. Law, we've checked your symptoms," said one of them as he looked down at me on the gurney. "There's no doubt about it. You're having a heart attack."

"No, I'm not," I protested, desperately hoping I was right and he was wrong.

"But you are," he insisted, both his colleagues nodding in agreement.

"Some bedside manner he's got," I thought to myself. "If I am having a heart attack, hearing about it sure isn't going to help."

The old saying that time flies when you're having fun has a corollary: time *crawls* when you're undergoing medical testing, especially if it includes an MRI. Yet, ironically, it was in the belly of that beast, when I had run out of physical space, that I discovered Covey's space, the "moment between stimulus and response." As I lay there, staring at a curved ceiling six inches from my nose, I realized that I had to choose between surrendering to well-founded fears and holding on to hope. I knew that my hope in God couldn't change my diagnosis, but it could certainly change my response.

Further tests proved the doctors wrong. The culprit in my chest was not a heart attack but viral pneumonia. And although it is a serious and potentially deadly illness, I was comforted at having faced only the shadow of death and not its angel.

"Yes," you say. "Your situation turned out fine, but mine didn't. And now I'm facing the biggest crisis of my life."

> *You have nothing to lose by choosing hope. God's Word, from cover to cover, challenges you to do so. I challenge you as well.*

That is all the more reason to hope in God. Remember, hope won't change a bad diagnosis or circumstance, but it *will* change you. I have already given you the testimony of Dr. Jerome Groopman, but it bears repeating:

- Within our brains are chemicals called endorphins and enkephalins, a natural form of morphine.
- Belief and expectation, cardinal components of hope, can block pain by releasing these chemicals.[14]
- Conversely, a sense of hopelessness causes the body to release fewer pain-deadening neurochemicals, creating a cycle that continues to increase pain and decrease hope.
- The first spark of hope can break that cycle and set off a chain reaction of shrinking pain and expanding hope.[15]

Add to this God-ordained physical process the promise (among hundreds of others) that "the eye of the LORD is on those who fear Him, on those who hope for His lovingkindness,"[16] and it should be clear that you are much wiser to hope in God than to give up on Him.

You have nothing to lose by choosing hope. God's Word, from cover to cover, challenges you to do so. I challenge you as well. I challenge you to realize that in reading these pages you have entered the "space," and there is only one exit: You must choose. And until you respond, *your moment of choice is always now.*

THE MIND-SET OF HOPE

I believe hope can become your normal way of looking at the world, so natural to you that you're not conscious of it until someone points it out with admiration (or envy). When that happens, you will have made a paradigm shift from the mind-set of fatalism to one of a continual, confident expectation of God's goodness. You will have *been* transformed by the renewing of your mind,[17] having integrated the mind-set of hope into your worldview.

I used the terms "paradigm shift" and "worldview" earlier in these pages; both might be new to you, so let me recap. Your worldview is the set of assumptions you make about reality. "We do not ordinarily see our own worldview, but we see everything else by looking through it," says Phillip Johnson, professor of law at the University of California at Berkeley.[18] Usually inherited rather than chosen, worldviews function virtually automatically, like a pair of glasses that you see through without thinking about them. In fact, it's normal to *not* think about your worldview but dangerous to *never* think about it, because it shapes your choices in life. A bad worldview will inevitably produce bad fruit.

The Bible is God's worldview, given to us specifically so that we will make it ours as well. And of course He sees the world from His throne, a far better perspective than our ground-level view. Moreover, since God has "raised us up with [Christ], and seated us with Him in the heavenly places in Christ Jesus,"[19] we get to see the big picture as God Himself sees it.

A truly biblical worldview will inevitably be characterized by hope, while a lack of hope is a sure indicator of a worldview uninformed, to some degree, by God's Word. Even the barest outline of a biblical worldview should cause hope to well up within you. For example:

- The earth is the Lord's, along with everyone and everything in it (Hebrews 1:3; Psalm 24:1).
- Man brought sin into the world, so God sent His Son, Jesus, to redeem the world—this means you!—by means of His atoning death and resurrection (John 3:16; Romans 5:8–9).

- Jesus possesses "all authority...in heaven and on earth" (Matthew 28:18).
- Jesus has restored your right standing with God (2 Corinthians 5:21) and your calling to "glorify God, and enjoy Him forever."[20]
- God has given you His Holy Spirit to guide you, His Word to fully equip you, and has ordained a pathway full of good works for you to walk in (John 16:8; 2 Timothy 3:16–17; Ephesians 2:10).
- Nothing can stop Jesus from building His church (Matthew 16:18).
- You and I are "joint heirs" with Christ, and we are inheriting the earth (Romans 8:17; Psalm 37:11; Matthew 5:5).
- Jesus will return in the same way He left to judge the living and the dead. On that day every knee will bow and every tongue will confess that Jesus Christ is Lord, to the glory of God the Father (Acts 1:11; Philippians 2:9–11).
- God will live amongst His people forever (Revelation 21:1–4).

In light of these incontestable facts, is it possible for a Christian to live without hope? Sure, just as it's possible for a billionaire to *choose* to live in the gutter or the owner of a grocery store to *choose* to starve to death. It's possible but absurd.

HARD CHOICES

Concerning the incarnation and crucifixion of Christ, author Phillip Yancey says, "God made himself weak for one purpose: to let human beings choose freely for themselves what to do with him."[21] That is the most amazing thing about grace: The omnipotent God chooses not to overrule our choices. He has chosen to make man free, even if it means a world of hurt, because the alternative is a world of biological machinery where the word *relationship* would describe nothing more than the cold intermeshing of gears, a world where *love* would be missing from the lexicon.

> *The Bible is God's worldview, given to us specifically so that we will make it ours as well.*

Men have balked at that divine decision for millennia. In fact, some, preferring a purposeless machine over having to grapple with the issue of evil, fight against their Creator all their lives. And none has been more conflicted than Albert Einstein, as authors Charles Colson and Nancy Pearcey reveal in their book *How Now Shall We Live?* Einstein once told a rabbi and two Christian pastors:

> "A real scientist...cannot for a moment entertain the idea of a being who interferes in the course of events."
>
> ..."If this personal being is omnipotent, then every event everywhere in the universe is his work— including every human action, every human thought, every human feeling....If he is the one ultimately responsible for our actions, then he is behind all the harm we do each other. In giving out punishments and rewards, he is in a way passing judgment on himself. God himself is the source of the very evil he supposedly judges!"

... [Einstein] had long nursed a smoldering anger about the suffering of the Jewish race through the centuries, and now ominous rumors were coming out of Germany. No, he could not accept the idea of a personal God who allowed such things to happen. And this afternoon's conversation had brought him no closer to an answer.[22]

Polish Jew Simon Wiesenthal also wrestled with Einstein's dilemma, but for even more personal reasons. The young architect lost eighty-nine relatives, including his mother and grandmother, at the hands of the Nazis. Indeed, after his own arrest he would have become number ninety if his attempt at suicide had succeeded. Instead, he found himself in a German prison camp, where one day he came face-to-face with a dying SS officer named Karl, who, tortured by guilt over his own brutality, now sought forgiveness from any Jew who might play the confessor.

Wiesenthal listened in silence as the man whispered through a hole in bandages that covered his face, recounting how his unit had herded three hundred Jews into a three-story house and then burned them to death. Philip Yancey picks up the story.

> Karl went on to describe other atrocities, but he kept circling back to the scene of that young boy with black hair and dark eyes, falling from a building, target practice for the SS rifles. "I am left here with my guilt," he concluded at last...
>
> "In the long nights while I have been waiting for death, time and time again I have longed to talk about it to a Jew and beg forgiveness from him. Only I didn't know whether there were any Jews left....I

know what I am asking is almost too much for you,
but without an answer I cannot die in peace."

… [Wiesenthal] stared out the window at the sunlit
courtyard. He looked at the eyeless heap of bandages
lying in the bed. He watched a bluebottle fly buzzing
the dying man's body, attracted by the smell.

"At last I made up my mind," Wiesenthal writes,
"and without a word I left the room."[23]

Wiesenthal would later be liberated by American forces, but the memory of that day haunted him for years like a ghost. Like Albert Einstein, it was not the world's evils that ultimately offended him but God's grace in the face of evil. Both men found it incomprehensible that a good God would rather allow human cruelty than remove human choice. Yet that unfathomable decision demonstrates just how paramount and precious is human liberty in God's economy. The truth is, what Yancey has termed God's "terrible insistence on human freedom" will *never* be understandable, because it is an aspect of His grace. That grace cannot be calculated or quantified but only received or rejected. It will, in fact, drive us to despair if we reject it or carry us to hope if we receive it.

That realization was what inspired a former slave trader named John Newton to pen an immortal lyric: "'Twas grace that taught my heart to fear, and grace my fears relieved."[24] Grace that does not frighten before it delights is grace not fully apprehended. Yet when it is caught, the way Newton caught it, grace will cause a kind of spiritual nuclear fission to take place as "fears" and "fears relieved" collide with such force that hope explodes the soul, leveling doubts, leaving despair in ruins, and filling every corner of the mind and emotions with the bright, glowing certainty of the goodness of God. Hope, in the words of physician Gerald May, "is a child of grace."[25]

CHOOSE HOPE

Nearly thirty-four hundred years ago an elderly leader stood before the tribal heads of the nation he had led for four decades to give his final, and certainly most important, national address. The great man was ready to hand over the reins of power to his successor, Joshua, some forty years his junior. But first, the old lion had some final words of wisdom for the people.

"I call heaven and earth to witness against you today," he intoned, "that I have set before you life and death, the blessing and the curse. So choose life in order that you may live, you and your descendants, by loving the LORD your God, by obeying His voice, and by holding fast to Him."[26]

It was that simple, really. Yes, the lessons had been long, and some of the laws complicated to the point of cryptic. But in the long run, said Moses, everything in Israel's covenant with God boiled down to a simple choice between "life and death, the blessing and the curse. So choose life…"

> *Grace will cause a spiritual nuclear fission to take place as "fears" and "fears relieved" collide with such force that hope explodes the soul.*

Moses knew that if the Israelites did not choose life, they were choosing death by default. Surrendering to the idea that "I have no choice" is a choice in itself. People *choose* to believe God has abandoned them. Even the victim of the most profound injustice, such as a child who has never known anything but abuse, can choose to cry out to God, who has promised to hear the cries of the oppressed.[27] No one is beyond redemption, because "everyone who calls on the name of the Lord will be saved."[28]

Some Christians find themselves in spiritual dry places and then conclude, "God must be trying to teach me something." Is that what the deserts of life are for, so the Almighty can teach us how to sweat? The prophet Hosea—who had every worldly excuse to be pessimistic—discovered a very different purpose for life's dry places. The Lord told him, "I will return [Israel's] vineyards to her and transform the Valley of Trouble into a gateway of hope."[29]

What perspective! *God leads His people into the desert to make the desert bloom!* If you're trapped in some "Valley of Trouble," this is great news for you. God has led you there because He wants to turn that valley into a *gateway of hope.*

In these pages Jim and I have given you a long and detailed look at hope, both real and counterfeit, inspirational and practical. Yet we've left certain aspects untouched. For example, we have not addressed every Christian's incredible hope of life after death—although we shall in a future volume—for one simple reason: *you need hope right where you are, and you need it now.*

> *Surrendering to the idea that "I have no choice" is a choice in itself. People choose to believe God has abandoned them.*

That is why we've brought you back to where you started: hope is a choice, and it is as stark and uncomplicated as the one Moses gave Israel all those years ago.

Choose hope.

THE DANCE OF HOPE

"Why show me this, if I am past all hope?"
—EBENEZER SCROOGE

WHEN CHARLES DICKENS published *A Christmas Carol* in 1843, he said in the preface that he had written it "to raise the Ghost of an Idea" with his readers and hoped it would "haunt their houses pleasantly, and no one wish to lay it" aside. But the legendary British writer surely could not have imagined that, more than 165 years later, his tale of the stingy old Ebenezer Scrooge and his three ghostly visitors would still pleasantly haunt millions of households around the world every Christmas in the form of books, stage productions, and numerous movies and television specials.

Recently, my wife Barbara and I toured Charles Dickens's London home and revisited his famous little book as well. Thumbing through its pages for the first time since my school days, I found myself riveted anew by his vivid prose, especially in describing his miserly main character.

> Oh, but he was tight-fist hand at the grindstone, Scrooge, a squeezing, wrenching, grasping, scraping,

clutching, covetous old sinner, hard and sharp as flint from which no steel had ever struck out generous fire, secret, self-contained, solitary as an oyster. The cold within him froze his old features, nipped his pointed nose, shriveled his cheeks, stiffened his gait, made his eyes red, his thin lips blue, and spoke out shrewdly in his grating voice...

Nobody ever stopped him in the street to say, "My dear Scrooge, how are you? When will you come to see me?" No beggars implored him to bestow money. No children asked him what time it was. No man or woman ever once in all of his life enquired the way to such and such a place of Scrooge.[1]

Ebenezer Scrooge's three visitors were the ghosts of Christmas past, present, and future. The first spirit took him back to his formative years, revisiting his days as a lonely schoolboy and then as an enterprising but increasingly isolated young businessman whose love for money eventually overruled all other loves in his life.

The Ghost of Christmas Present gave Scrooge a look at the current holiday celebrations taking place around his hometown, including a peek into the happy home of employee Bob Cratchit, whose poverty was largely the old moneylender's fault. He watched as Bob, the kindhearted husband and father, insisted that the family toast the old skinflint, even though "a shadow was cast over the party for a full five minutes." And he saw Tiny Tim, the Cratchit's stricken child whose heart was as generous as his father's, but whose life would soon end without medical care that was beyond the family's meager means.

At length Scrooge was confronted by a third spirit, a black, shrouded specter who led him, without words, across town and time to a Christmas not yet come. Gliding silently through the streets, the increasingly frightened old man could hear the hiss of whispered conversation, the same one on every set of lips, it seemed. In the city's heart, businessmen were discussing the death of someone they clearly did not mourn. Over on the bad side of town, where the gossip continued in more colorful terms, his own housekeeper hawked her master's bed linens, blankets, and curtains in a makeshift street market. The shadowy angel also whisked him into, and through, the Cratchit home, where the family mourned their now deceased Tiny Tim. Finally, after terminating their journey at an overgrown churchyard cemetery, the spirit pointed Scrooge to an obviously neglected tombstone. And as the terrified man knelt to brush aside the weeds, the horrible truth of his own destiny was at last revealed.

> Scrooge crept towards it, trembling as he went; and following the finger, read upon the stone of the neglected grave his own name, EBENEZER SCROOGE.
>
> "Am I that man who lay upon the bed?" he cried, upon his knees.
>
> The finger pointed from the grave to him, and back again.
>
> "No, Spirit! Oh no, no!"
>
> The finger still was there.
>
> "Spirit!" he cried, tightly clutching at its robe, "hear me. I am not the man I was. I will not be the man I must have been but for this intercourse. *Why show me this, if I am past all hope?*"[2]

You know the rest of the story. Ebenezer grabbed the spirit's rigid black arm and pled for his life, only to awaken clinging to his own bedpost. Seeing his blanket and curtains still in place, he began to rejoice that he was alive after all. Dancing about on one leg as he tried to pull on his pants, Scrooge was giddy with the knowledge that he still had time to change—still had time to bless the people whose lives he had *humbugged* for so many years. The story ends with him dancing through town to the Cratchit home, along the way patting startled children on the head, giving a huge gift to equally startled citizens trying to raise money for the poor, and finally blessing Bob Cratchit and his family with not only a gigantic turkey for dinner but also a gigantic raise at work.

> *Like Scrooge, you can still choose to hope, not only for yourself but also for your family and everyone else in your world. The choice is yours, and the time to choose is now.*

Ebenezer Scrooge had gone to bed a sinner and arisen a saint for one reason: he had asked, and answered, the most important question of his heretofore miserable life. *"Why show me this, if I am past all hope?"* He had realized that if he would change his present, he could change his future.

HOPE FOR YOU

Think back on what you've read in these pages and ask yourself Ebenezer's question: *Why show me this, if I am past all hope?* The answer, of course, is that it is not too late for you. Like Scrooge, you can still choose to hope, not only for yourself but also for your family and everyone else in your world. *The choice is yours, and the time to choose is now.*

For a moment, forget that you are reading, and imagine that you and I are sitting face-to-face in your favorite getaway. Look me in the eye. I'm asking you to make a permanent commitment to a lifestyle of hope, no matter what, even if at first you see no apparent change in your situation. *Are you willing to choose the paradigm of hope right now, to start saying about yourself what God says about you?* I will assume your answer is yes.

Look at the Declarations of Hope below, and repeat them aloud, beginning each with either "I will stop saying" or "I will start saying." Talking aloud might seem a bit strange, since you are probably either reading alone or next to a sleeping spouse. But as we shall see later, saying them with your mouth is important. Now, go ahead and make your declarations.

DECLARATIONS OF HOPE	
I will stop saying:	I will start saying:
My situation is hopeless.	I am confident in the goodness of God. There is hope for me.
I hate waking up in the morning.	The Lord's mercies are new every morning, and His faithfulness is great. Therefore I will hope in Him.[3]
My bills are overwhelming; I'm even afraid to answer the phone.	My God will supply all my needs according to His riches in glory in Christ Jesus.[4]
I don't deserve another chance.	I will draw near with confidence to God's throne, where I can receive mercy and find grace to help in my time of need.[5]
Nothing ever works out for me.	I believe God has plans for me, for good and not for evil, to give me a future and a hope.[6]
My father did this to me.	I am a new creation in Christ Jesus. My past has been wiped out; everything has become new.[7]
My country is too far gone; I can't make a difference.	I will humble myself and pray and seek God's face, turning away from wickedness, so that God will hear from heaven, forgive our sins, and heal our land.[8]

DECLARATIONS OF HOPE	
I will stop saying:	I will start saying:
My problems are too big to solve.	Nothing is impossible with God.[9]
God has forgotten me. I feel so alone in the world.	I am the apple of God's eye; He hides me in the shadow of His wings.[10]
I'm damaged goods. Who would ever want to marry me?	Therefore there is now no condemnation for me, because I am in Christ Jesus.[11]
I can't raise these children by myself.	I can do all things through Him who strengthens me.[12]
My professor makes a fool of me.	Men will see my good works and glorify my Father who is in heaven.[13]
I'll never break free of this habit.	Yet in all these things we are more than conquerors through Him who loved us.[14]
I'll never get well.	By His stripes I was healed.[15]
It's not my fault. I'm the victim here. I've been cheated, abused, ripped off.	I have worked harder, been put in jail more often, been whipped times without number, and faced death again and again.... If I must boast, I would rather boast about the things that show how weak I am.[16]

If you are near a computer, please stop reading for a moment and go to www.thehopehabit.tv to view a short video of encouragement from me to you. Then, before you resume reading, make sure to bookmark the Web site as a place for future resources on living a "hope-full" life.

HEART ON FIRE

In reading your new Declarations of Hope, you might have thought they sounded familiar. In fact, every positive statement you just made about yourself was a personalized version of one or more verses of the Holy Scriptures. Why use passages from the Bible as an antidote to hopelessness? *Because the cure for what you say about your situation is what God says about your situation!*

Have you ever asked yourself, "What would Jesus do?" Well, I can tell you what He *did*. At the outset of His ministry, the Lord stated quite plainly that He had come "to bring Good News to the poor... to proclaim that captives will be released, that the blind will see, that the oppressed will be set free, and that the time of the Lord's favor has come."[17] Then, for the better part of three years, everywhere He went, He told a world full of mixed-up people what God's Word said about them. From birth, His mission was to bring hope to a human race without hope.

Jesus accomplished this by continually explaining and personally fulfilling the Scriptures. Remember, for example, the story I referenced earlier about the two men walking from Jerusalem to the nearby village of Emmaus? Like so many of their Jewish countrymen, they had been hoping Jesus was Israel's long-promised Messiah, but they had watched that hope die two days earlier with His crucifixion. On this late Sunday afternoon, the resurrected Jesus joined them while they walked, but for some reason they failed to recognize Him.

> *The cure for what you say about your situation is what God says about your situation!*

Look at how the Lord stirred hope in these discouraged disciples. "Then beginning with Moses and with all the prophets," Luke wrote, "He explained to them the things concerning Himself in all the Scriptures,"[18] to which they subsequently responded, "Were not our hearts burning within us while He was speaking to us on the road, while He was explaining the Scriptures to us?"[19]

Jesus set their hearts on fire with words—words from the same mouth that eons earlier had commanded, "Let there be light," and set the stars ablaze. He taught them from the Scriptures, because He knew that they were the cure for hopelessness. St. Paul later shared this insight with Rome's first congregation, telling them, "Whatever was written in earlier times was written for our instruction, so that through perseverance and the encouragement of the Scriptures we might have hope."[20]

The Bible is no mere history book, collection of wise sayings, or set of mysteries waiting to be decoded by twenty-first century computers. As my friend David Nielson can attest, God's Word is "living and active and sharper than any two-edged sword."[21] David is a Pakistani pastor who spends much of his time helping refugees from nearby Afghanistan. One day a Pashtun tribal elder came to him and held out the Bible David had given him a week earlier.

"What is it about this book?" he pleaded. "Every time I open it, I see a vision of a Lamb standing by a glorious throne in front of millions and millions of people. When I close the book it goes away, and when I open it, it comes back. What is this?"

David opened the Bible to Revelation, chapter 5, and showed the refugee the scene in his vision, convincing the man that his "book" was truly God's Word. That episode paved the way for David to open the rest of Scripture to him, guiding him to faith in Christ Jesus. The most fascinating aspect of the story is that God gave the Afghan tribesman a vision that directed him to the Bible rather than showing everything to him supernaturally. This indicates just how important the Scriptures really are.

IN THE FLESH

Far from being a metaphor, the term "living and active" is literal. "The Word became human," explained St. John, "and made his home among us. He was full of unfailing love and faithfulness. And we have seen his glory, the glory of the Father's one and only Son."[22] Jesus was and is the full expression of God in bodily form, the "Word made flesh." That is why He said, "He who has seen Me has seen the Father."[23] Yet, despite this fact, and despite the miracles He performed, the Lord's continual emphasis was on revealing God through the Scriptures; i.e., on *hearing* more than on seeing. This is why, although the Pashtun elder had seen Jesus as a "Lamb standing by a glorious throne," the Scriptures were necessary to reveal the Lamb's identity.

The physical incarnation of God's Word took place during an encounter between the angel Gabriel and a Jewish virgin named Mary. Their conversation, recorded in the Gospel of Luke, has been replayed in so many church dramas and films that it is easy to overlook its details. "You *will* conceive in your womb and bear a Son," Gabriel said. "The Holy Spirit *will* come upon you, and the power of the Most High *will* overshadow you."[24] The future tense indicates Mary had not yet conceived. Yet immediately after the angel's departure a few verses later, Mary is spoken of as pregnant. This leaves one obvious moment when the Word of God became flesh in Mary's womb.

> And Mary said, "Behold, the bondslave of the Lord;
> may it be done to me according to your word." And
> the angel departed from her.[25]

The Word of God came alive in the young girl's womb as soon as she believed the words of the angel and replied, "May

207

it be done to me according to your word." In that one miraculous moment, the whole world changed, and a new human life was added to the earth's population. His name was Jesus, and He was alive—then and there—because of Mary's words.

LEARNING BY MOUTH

The Bible word *angel* simply means "messenger." When a messenger delivers God's Word to an unbeliever, that unbeliever is called upon to believe in his heart and confess with his mouth that Jesus is Lord.[26] At that moment Jesus comes alive in a human heart. It is the miracle of Mary once again.

Notice that in Romans 10:9, the heart and mouth are directly connected. I have described this connection in an earlier book.

> The Scriptures consistently demonstrate a connection between the mouth and the heart. Jesus said in Matthew 12:34, "...For out of the abundance of the heart the mouth speaks." It is inevitable. Whatever fills the heart eventually will be spoken, because *the mouth is the faucet of the heart.*
>
> Does that statement strike you in a good way or a fearful one? If your heart already abounds with God's Word, it probably gladdens you to read it. But if your heart is filled with fear, and your mind is gripped with worry, it probably just adds to the pressure. Truth cuts both ways...
>
> God created the world with His Word (see John 1), and still rules His creation accordingly (see Hebrews 1:3). He also created man in His image, to rule the earth under Him by obeying and enforcing that Word. Therefore if Satan can turn man's heart and

capture his tongue, he usurps man's dominion over the earth.

That is why your mouth is ground zero in the war for the universe. Once your heart is captured, the devil knows your mouth will speak from its abundance. *Whoever controls the mouth controls the man.*[27]

In order to make the paradigm shift to hope, it is necessary for your words about yourself to start lining up with God's words about you. *Your mouth is where that shift begins.* The key is to continually conform your words to God's Word, until your automatic response in any situation is one that agrees with what He says. This obviously involves both mediation and memorization. In English we refer to this process as "learning by heart," but the Hebrew phrase "learning by mouth" is more accurate. You didn't learn "Mary had a little lamb" as a child by silently thinking the words and melody. No, you sang them aloud, over and over. Likewise, you remember your multiplication tables today because you repeated them *ad infinitum* in the second grade. You learned them by mouth.

> *Your mouth is ground zero in the war for the universe.*

YOUR CONFESSION OF HOPE

Earlier in this chapter, you read aloud several Declarations of Hope, which are actually personalized paraphrases of selected scriptures. In the Bible, this sort of speech is called the *confession* of hope. I use the term *declaration* for clarity's sake since most people associate the word *confession* with an admission of wrongdoing. But *confess* is actually more precise, because the word means "to speak the same." When you confess the truth, you are merely aligning your words with the facts of the matter. With this in mind, look at Hebrews 10:23, which encourages us to "hold fast the confession of our hope without wavering, for He who promised is faithful."

The imagery in that sentence is almost nautical. When life comes at you like a storm, the hope-filled words of your mouth will steer you through, as though your tongue were a rudder to keep you on course. Actually, this very metaphor was used by the apostle James, who called the tongue a "very small rudder" that steers the whole person.[28]

But how does holding fast to your confession of hope keep you from crashing? Is it mind over matter? Not at all. The rest of the verse explains why you must hold fast without wavering: "For He who promised is faithful." *God is faithful to fulfill the promises that you continue confessing in hope.*

EBENEZER'S DANCE

I have repeatedly defined hope as "the confident expectation of the goodness of God." I trust that by now you understand clearly why I say "confident" rather than "tentative." There is nothing uncertain about hope in God, no caution of the sort we might exercise when having to rely on some frail, fallible friend. St. Paul even talked about "exulting" in hope, because you have "been justified by faith, [and] have peace with God through our Lord Jesus Christ."[29]

> *When life comes at you like a storm, the hope-filled words of your mouth will steer you through, as though your tongue were a rudder to keep you on course.*

Isn't that a fitting description of what took place in the allegorical life of Ebenezer Scrooge? The old man, forgiven and at peace with God and his fellow man, exulted in hope as he danced around his bedroom, out the door, and through the streets. His mind and heart had changed—*really* changed. He had made a paradigm shift from bitterness and despair to joy and hope.

Look at the new Scrooge: His talents were the same, but his use of them was entirely different. For example, he was still a schemer, but oh what a schemer he now was!

> "I'll send it [the large turkey] to Bob Cratchit's!" whispered Scrooge, rubbing his hands, and splitting with a laugh. "He sha'n't know who sends it. It's twice the size of Tiny Tim."[30]

Scrooge's new mind-set also opened his eyes to small blessings he had never seen before, to blessings not even nicer folk would notice.

> The hand in which he wrote the address was not a steady one, but write it he did, somehow, and went down-stairs to open the street door, ready for the coming of the poulterer's man. As he stood there, waiting his arrival, the knocker caught his eye.
>
> "I shall love it, as long as I live!" cried Scrooge, patting it with his hand, "I scarcely ever look at it before....What an honest expression it has in its face! It's a wonderful knocker!"[31]

You might not be dancing or kissing doorbells just yet, but there is no reason in the world why such boisterous hope and joy cannot be yours. Indeed, the Bible recommends that we "hold fast our confidence and the boast of our hope firm until the end."[32] Furthermore, you need not wait to boast until you think you've "turned the corner" or that you "see the light at the end of the tunnel." Your hope is based on the faithfulness of Jesus Christ, which means that right now, right there in the pit of despair, with no end of trouble in sight, you can begin boasting *in Him*.

Now is the time to make your confession of hope, to take what God's Word says about you, and to say it about yourself, just as I showed you earlier in the Declarations of Hope chart. To that end, please seize the opportunity I present to you on the following page. And as you turn the page, make the shift from old to new, from your words to God's Word. *It is time to make your Vow of Hope!*

> *Right there in the pit of despair, with no end of trouble in sight, you can begin boasting of your hope in Him.*

My Vow of Hope

I, _____

(YOUR NAME), on

_____(DATE),

do hereby make the following solemn vow
before Almighty God: From this moment
forward and forever, I dedicate myself to
the habit of hope, to live my life in constant,
confident expectation of the goodness of God.
I believe it is not too late for me, that God has
plans for me, for my good and not for evil, to
give me a future and a hope. I fully believe
that by the power of the Holy Spirit I will
learn to abound in hope. From this moment
forward, I am resolved to set my hope fully on
the fact that God is causing all things to work
together for good in my life.

NOTES

Chapter 1—Whatever Happened to Hope?

1. David Augsburger, *When Enough Is Enough* (Ventura, CA: Regal Books, 1984), 10.
2. Hillary Mayell, "India's 'Untouchables' Face Violence, Discrimination," National Geographic News, June 2, 2003, http://news.nationalgeographic.com/news/2003/06/0602_030602_untouchables.html (accessed November 23, 2009).
3. John Paul II, *Ecclesia in Europe* (n.p.: n.d.), 2, as quoted in George Wiegel, *The Cube and the Cathedral* (New York: Basic Books, 2006), 117.
4. Ibid., 3, in Wiegel, *The Cube and the Cathedral*, 117.
5. There is, for example, much good taking place in Iraq at this writing (I have seen it with my own eyes). Yet, media bias against the war dictates negative coverage only.
6. David Kinnaman and Gabe Lyons, *unChristian* (Grand Rapids: Baker Books, 2007), 26–27.
7. Rick Warren, *The Purpose-Driven Life* (Grand Rapids: Zondervan, 2002), 36.
8. Fellow senior Larry Dalton and I founded our music group Living Sound while we were students at Oral Roberts University. Our idea was a radical one in 1969: combine contemporary music with preaching to present the gospel of Jesus Christ around the world. From 1969–1987 we fielded as many as four teams at a time and presented the gospel in dozens of nations around the world.
9. Augsburger, *When Enough Is Enough*, 25, 27.
10. Matthew 28:19–20.
11. Brother Andrew, *And God Changed His Mind* (Old Tappan: Chosen Books, 1990), 23–24.
12. J. I. Packer, *Never Beyond Hope* (Downers Grove: IVP Books, 2000), 20.
13. *Tithe* is the biblical practice of giving the first and best 10 percent of one's increase (net income) to God.
14. "Less than one out of every ten regular attenders of Christian churches gives 10% or more of their income—a 'tithe'—to their church. A majority of teenagers attend a Christian church today, but only one-third is likely to do so once they reach adulthood. The persecution delivered by the terrorist attacks has produced no increase in spiritual practices, such as attending worship services, reading the Bible, praying, or serving the needy. Giving levels have actually decreased this year. In fact, not even half of Americans indicated that their faith had been an important factor in helping them process the effects of the terrorist attacks." —The Barna Group, "Barna Identifies Seven Paradoxes Regarding America's

Faith," Barna.org, December 17, 2002, http://www.barna.org/
barna-update/article/5-barna-update/87-barna-identifies-seven
-paradoxes-regarding-americas-faith (accessed November 19,
2009).

15. C. Peter Wagner, *Churches That Pray* (Ventura, CA: Regal Books,
2003), 42.

16. Ibid., 43–44.

17. Brother Andrew, *And God Changed His Mind*, 37.

18. "Because you are sons, God has sent forth the Spirit of His Son into
our hearts, crying, 'Abba! Father!' Therefore you are no longer a
slave, but a son; and if a son, then an heir through God" (Galatians
4:6–7).

19. Peter F. Drucker, "Managing Knowledge Means Managing Onself,"
Leader to Leader 16, Spring 2000, 8–10, as quoted in Stephen R.
Covey, *The 8th Habit* (New York: Free Press, 2004), 12.

20. "For I know the plans I have for you, declares the LORD, plans for
welfare and not for evil, to give you a future and a hope" (Jeremiah
29:11, ESV).

21. W. E. Vine, *Vine's Complete Expository Dictionary of Old and New
Testament Words* (Nashville: Thomas Nelson, 1996), s.v., "hope."

22. Romans 8:28.

23. "And not only this, but we also exult in our tribulations [troubles],
knowing that tribulation brings about perseverance; and perseverance, proven character; and proven character, hope" (Romans
5:3–4).

24. 2 Timothy 1:7, NKJV.

25. Frederic Golden, "The Worst and the Best," *TIME*, October 16,
2000, http://www.time.com/time/magazine/article/0,9171,998209,00
.html (accessed November 23, 2009).

26. Gabriel Fackre, as quoted in Augsburger, *When Enough Is Enough*,
155.

CHAPTER 2—THE MEANING OF HOPE

1. Colossians 1:27.

2. 1 Corinthians 13:13.

3. Romans 15:13.

4. 1 Thessalonians 5:8.

5. Hebrews 6:19.

6. 1 Corinthians 15:14.

7. Terry Law with Jim Gilbert, *The Power of Praise and Worship*
(Shippensburg, PA: Destiny Image, 2008).

8. Isaiah 61:3, NKJV.

9. Jonah 2:9–10.

10. Law with Gilbert, *The Power of Praise and Worship*.

11. U.S. Census Bureau Population Division, "U.S. Census Bureau
Population Estimates by Demographic Characteristics. Table 2:
Annual Estimates of the Population by Selected Age Groups and Sex

for the United States: April 1, 2000 to July 1, 2004 (NC-EST2004-02)," Census.gov, June 9, 2005, http://www.census .gov/popest/national/asrh/, referenced in National Institute of Mental Health, "The Numbers Count: Mental Disorders in America," 2008, http://www.nimh.nih.gov/health/publications/the -numbers-count-mental-disorders-in-america/index.shtml# Dysthymic (accessed November 23, 2009).

12. R. C. Kessler, W. T. Chiu, O. Demler, and E. E. Walters, "Prevalence, Severity, and Comorbidity of Twelve-Month DSM-IV Disorders in the National Comorbidity Survey Replication (NCS-R)," *Archives of General Psychiatry* 62, no. 6 (June 2005): 617–627.

13. World Health Organization, "Depression," WHO.int, http://www .who.int/mental_health/management/depression/definition/en/ (accessed November 19, 2009).

14. Deuteronomy 30:19.

15. Stephen Mansfield, *Derek Prince: A Biography* (Lake Mary, FL: Charisma House, 2005), 24, 102.

16. Tracy Corrigan, "Be Wary of Popping the Pill Question," *Telegraph*, September 29, 2009, http://www.telegraph.co.uk/finance/comment/ tracycorrigan/6241564/Be-wary-of-popping-the-pill-question.html (accessed December 29, 2009).

17. 1 John 4:4.

18. Romans 8:37, NKJV.

19. Jerome Groopman, *The Anatomy of Hope* (New York: Random House, 2005), 198–199. Used by permission of Random House Inc.

20. J. I. Packer and Carolyn Nystrom, *Never Beyond Hope* (Downers Grove, IL: Intervarsity Press, 2000), 15.

21. 1 Thessalonians 5:8.

22. Romans 10:10.

23. Romans 15:4.

24. Derek Prince, *Faith to Live By* (New Kensington, PA: Whitaker House, 1977), 20.

25. Genesis 37.

26. 1 Corinthians 2:12–13, 16.

27. Covey, *The 8th Habit*, 32.

28. James 1:22.

29. Romans 15:13.

CHAPTER 3—THE INVITATION TO HOPE

1. QuoteDB.com, "Victor Hugo Quotes," http://www.quotedb.com/ quotes/239 (accessed November 19, 2009).

2. Lewis Smedes, *Keeping Hope Alive* (Nashville: Thomas Nelson, 1998), 67.

3. Avalon Project at Yale Law School, "Declaration of Israel's Independence 1978, Issued at Tel Aviv on May 14, 1948 (5th of Iyar, 5708)," http://avalon.law.yale.edu/20th_century/israel.asp (accessed November 23, 2009).

4. Smedes, *Keeping Hope Alive*, 19.
5. Alex Bein, as quoted in Louis Lipsky, introduction to *The Jewish State* by Theodor Herzl (New York: Dover Publications, 1988), 13, http://www.gutenberg.org/files/25282/25282-h/25282-h.htm (accessed November 23, 2009).
6. Theodor Herzl, *The Jewish State* (n.p.: Voasha Publishing, 2008), 80–81.
7. Groopman, *The Anatomy of Hope*, 208. Used by permission of Random House Inc.
8. Ibid., xvi.
9. Ibid., 159.
10. Ibid., 155–156.
11. Ibid.
12. Jerome Groopman, *The Measure of Our Days* (New York: Penguin, 1998).
13. Jerome Groopman, *Second Opinions* (New York: Penguin, 2001).
14. Groopman, *The Anatomy of Hope*, 162.
15. Ibid., 170.
16. Ibid., 179.
17. Ibid., 190.
18. Viktor Frankl, *Man's Search for Meaning* (New York: Penguin, 2001), 15.
19. Douglas Wilson, *The Deluded Atheist* (Powder Springs, GA: American Vision Press, 2008), Amazon Kindle e-book, location 728.
20. Luke 23:42.
21. Romans 15:13.

Chapter 4—Stolen Hopes

1. Song of Solomon 2:15.
2. Recounted by Betsy Thraves in conversation with author, June 2009.
3. Song of Solomon 2:15.
4. Jeremiah 29:11.
5. Steven K. Scott, *Simple Steps to Impossible Dreams* (New York: Fireside, 1998), 34.
6. Ibid., chapter 4.
7. Ibid., chapter 5.
8. Ibid., chapter 6.
9. Ibid., chapter 7.
10. Ibid., chapter 8.
11. Ibid., chapter 9.
12. Deuteronomy 29:9.
13. Scott, *Simple Steps to Impossible Dreams*, 50.
14. Andy Stanley, *Visioneering* (Sisters, OR: Multnomah Publishing, 1999), 110–111.
15. Scott, *Simple Steps to Impossible Dreams*, 62.
16. Philippians 3:14, KJV.
17. QuoteDB.com, "John Lennon Quotes," http://www.quotedb.com/

quotes/2005 (accessed November 23, 2009).

18. See Romans 4:18.
19. Scott, *Simple Steps to Impossible Dreams*, 92–93.
20. Romans 12:2.
21. 1 Thessalonians 5:24.
22. J. I. Packer, *Never Beyond Hope* (Downers Grove, IL: Intervarsity Press, 2000), 18.
23. Judges 6:12.
24. Judges 6:27.
25. 1 Samuel 13:14.
26. John 1:42.
27. Luke 22:55–62.
28. Matthew 14:28–31.
29. James 1:23–25.
30. 1 John 4:4.

Chapter 5—Illusions of Hope

1. Brainyquote.com, "Joseph Addison Quotes," http://www.brainyquote.com/quotes/quotes/j/josephaddi148379.html (accessed November 10, 2009).
2. See Jake Halpern, *Fame Junkies: The Hidden Truths Behind America's Favorite Addiction* (New York: Houghton Mifflin, 2007).
3. CBS/AP, "Family: Michael Jackson Had a Will," CBSNews.com, June 30, 2009, http://www.cbsnews.com/stories/2009/06/30/entertainment/main5125862.shtml (accessed December 17, 2009).
4. George Wiegel, *The Cube and the Cathedral: Europe, America, and Politics Without God* (New York: Basic Books, 2005), 118.
5. Ibid.
6. As recently as 2005, eighteen nations in Europe were experiencing negative birth rates (more deaths than births) and no European nation had a replacement birth rate of 2.1 children per family. In fact, France came closest with 1.89 births per family, but that figure is inflated by very high birth rates amongst Muslim immigrants. As one author has said, Europe is becoming Eurabia. SOURCE: Nicholas Eberstadt, "The Emptying of Russia," *Washington Post*, February 13, 2004, A27, in Wiegel, *The Cube and the Cathedral*, 21; Mark Steyne, *America Alone* (Washington: Regnery Publishing, 2006), 54.
7. 1 Corinthians 15:19, NKJV.
8. Jim Dailey, "A Conversation With Ravi Zacharias," *Decision*, March 2002, http://www.billygraham.org/DMag_Article.asp?ArticleID=75 (accessed December 29, 2009).
9. Augsburger, *When Enough Is Enough*, 14.
10. Ibid.
11. Ibid., 20.
12. Ibid., 60.
13. Ibid., 18.

14. Ibid.
15. Ibid., 134–135.
16. See 1 Thessalonians 5:8.
17. Isaiah 6:5.
18. Philippians 2:5, NKJV.
19. 2 Timothy 3:16–17.
20. Hebrews 11:27, NLT.
21. Romans 15:13.

CHAPTER 6—WHEN HOPE DIES

1. ThinkExist.com, "Friedrich Nietzsche Quotes," http://thinkexist .com/quotation/hope_is_the_worst_of_evils-for_it_prolongs_ the/176293.html (accessed November 10, 2009).
2. Viktor E. Frankl, *Man's Search for Meaning* (New York: Pocket Books, 1984), 95.
3. Ibid., 96.
4. Ibid., 36–37.
5. See Romans 1:20–23.
6. Numbers 14:2–3.
7. 1 Kings 19:14.
8. See 1 Kings 19.
9. Hebrews 11:19.
10. Romans 4:18.
11. Mark 10:27, NKJV.
12. Isaiah 60:2–3.
13. Matthew 5:16.
14. 1 Peter 1:3.

CHAPTER 7—THE VOICE OF HOPE

1. John 1:42.
2. Genesis 6:5.
3. Acts 13:22, NKJV.
4. According to IndexMundi.com, Iraq's 2008 birth rate hovered just above 30 per 1,000, nearly twice that of neighboring Iran; IndexMundi.com, "Country Comparison: Birth Rate," http:// indexmundi.com/g/r.aspx?c=iz&v=25 (accessed November 19, 2009).
5. Romans 15:13. It is interesting that the two ingredients of "joy and peace in believing" produced a third one: hope!
6. Philippians 3:13–14.
7. Proverbs 18:21.
8. Luke 19:9.
9. See Numbers 5:11–31.
10. John 8:11.
11. Luke 23:42–43.
12. Acts 4:13, KJV.
13. John 7:49.
14. Robert E. Coleman, *The Master Plan of Evangelism* (Grand Rapids, MI: Revell, 1993), 91.

15. John 1:42.
16. Luke 22:31–34, NLT.
17. Matthew 26:74.
18. Luke 22:60–61.
19. Revelation 1:14; 19:12.
20. Romans 8:1.
21. 1 John 1:7.
22. Romans 8:28.
23. Romans 12:4–5.
24. Romans 8:37.
25. Genesis 1:27.
26. Ephesians 1:6, NKJV.
27. Isaiah 53:5, NKJV.
28. Hebrews 4:16.
29. Matthew 5:13–14.
30. Matthew 5:16.
31. Philippians 1:6.
32. Judges 6:14.
33. Ephesians 2:10
34. Romans 8:38–39.
35. Mark 10:13–15; Luke 18:15–17, NLT
36. Oral Roberts, *When You See The Invisible You Can Do The Impossible* (Shippensburg, PA: Destiny Image, 2002), 18.
37. Ibid., 20–21.
38. Ibid.

CHAPTER 8—THE PROMISES OF HOPE

1. Romans 15:4.
2. Luke 23:55–56.
3. Luke 24:5–7.
4. Luke 24:8.
5. Luke 18:31–34.
6. Luke 24:11.
7. Luke 24:16. See the remainder of Luke 24 for the full passage described in this section. Italics in Scripture quotes in text are added emphasis by author.
8. Genesis 22:18.
9. Luke 19:11. Read the remainder of this chapter for further insight as to how the kingdom of God comes about.
10. See Mark 10:35–40; Luke 22:24–30.
11. Luke 24:27, emphasis added.
12. Genesis 22:18.
13. 1 Peter 1:23.
14. Psalm 22:16–18, NKJV.
15. Psalm 69:20–21.
16. Isaiah 50:6.

17. 1 Peter 1:10–11, emphasis added.
18. 1 Peter 1:12.
19. 1 Peter 1:13.
20. The odds against one man fulfilling hundreds of ancient prophecies are truly astronomical, having been calculated as high as 1 followed by 157 zeroes.
21. 2 Peter 1:21, ESV.
22. John 16:13.
23. Romans 15:4.
24. Abraham means "father of a multitude."
25. Genesis 12:1–3.
26. Lewis Smedes, *Keeping Hope Alive* (Nashville: Thomas Nelson, Inc., 1998), 110–112. Used by permission.
27. Ibid.
28. Romans 4:19.
29. Romans 4:18.
30. Genesis 17:5, NKJV.
31. 1 Corinthians 15:14.
32. Acts 2:25–28, emphasis added. See also Psalm 16.
33. Smedes, *Keeping Hope Alive*.
34. Ibid.

CHAPTER 9—THE HELMET OF HOPE

1. National Highway Traffic Safety Administration, "Motorcycle Helmet Use Laws," Traffic Safety Facts, January 2006, http://www.nhtsa.dot.gov/staticfiles/DOT/NHTSA/Rulemaking/Articles/Associated%20Files/03%20Motorcycle%20Helmet%20Use.pdf (accessed December 29, 2009).
2. Revelation 12:10.
3. For more information, see the author's book *The Power of Praise and Worship* (Shippensburg, PA: Destiny Image, 2008).
4. Ephesians 6:13–17.
5. 1 Corinthians 13:13.
6. For a more comprehensive treatment of the subject matter in this chapter, see Terry Law, *The Fight of Every Believer* (Tulsa, OK: Harrison House, Inc., 2006).
7. Luke 4:14.
8. Augsburger, *When Enough Is Enough*, 10, 12.
9. Mark 1:15.
10. Ephesians 5:26.
11. Gretchen Smith, "My Story," Livrite.com, http://www.livrite.com/eds/story.htm (accessed November 19, 2009). Used by permission.
12. Ibid.
13. Psalm 119:11.
14. Hebrews 4:12.
15. Visit Gretchen Smith's "Renovation" Web site at http://livrite.com/renovation (accessed November 19, 2009).

16. Gretchen Smith, "Where Do Eating Disorders Come From?" Livrite
.com, http://livrite.com/renovation/wdedcf.htm (accessed November
19, 2009).
17. 2 Corinthians 7:10.
18. Covey, *The 8th Habit*, 41.
19. Jeremiah 17:9.
20. Ezekiel 28:15.
21. Terry Boyd, *Stars and Stripes*, European edition, October 31, 2004,
http://www.stripes.com/article.asp?section=104&article=25223
(accessed November 12, 2009).
22. 1 Thessalonians 5:8.
23. Romans 8:28.
24. Psalm 23:6, NKJV.

CHAPTER 10—THE EYES OF HOPE

1. *Man of La Mancha*, DVD, directed by Arthur Hiller (1972; n.p.:
MGM/UA Home Entertainment, 2004).
2. Georges Hormuz Sada, *Saddam's Secrets* (Nashville, TN: Thomas
Nelson, 2009).
3. Carl Sagan, *Cosmos* (n.p.: Ballatine Books, 1985), 1.
4. Romans 5:5.
5. 2 Corinthians 4:18.
6. Acts 17:24–27.
7. See 2 Kings 6:12–17.
8. For more information on this subject, see my book *The Truth About
Angels* (Lake Mary, FL: Charisma House, 2006).
9. Mark 4:24–25, AMP.
10. See Numbers 13.
11. Proverbs 13:12.
12. Numbers 13:33, NKJV.
13. Numbers 14:7–9.
14. Hebrews 11:27.
15. They are joined by fully complicit educational and political
establishments. As I write, the president of the United States is
dramatically expanding the American welfare bureaucracy, while
proposing to lower the tax deduction taxpayers can claim for
monies donated to churches and charities.
16. FOXNews report, October 8, 2009.
17. Patrick Johnstone, *The Church is Bigger Than You Think* (Fearn,
Ross-shire, GB: Christian Focus Publications, 1998), 114.
18. Pew Forum on Religion & Public Life, "Mapping the Global Muslim
Population," October 2009, http://pewforum.org/docs/?DocID=450
(accessed December 30, 2009).
19. See Psalm 110; Matthew 22:44; Mark 12:36; Luke 20:42; Acts 2:34;
Hebrews 1:13.
20. See Acts 17.
21. Philippians 2:5, NKJV.

22. Philippians 4:8.
23. Isabelle Barker, "Engendering Charismatic Economies: Pentecostalism, Global Political Economy, and the Crisis of Social Reproduction," paper presented at the annual meeting of the American Political Science Association, Marriott Wardman Park, Omni Shoreham, Washington Hilton, Washington DC, September 1, 2005, http://www.allacademic.com/meta/p39879_index.html (accessed November 13, 2009). More information can also be obtained from, among others, the Internet Web sites of Church Growth Today, Glenmary Research Center, Pew Forum on Religion & Public Life, World Christian Database, and *Foreign Policy* magazine.
24. For more information, visit http://www.rezasafa.com.
25. Daniel 4:25, NKJV.
26. Psalm 110:2.
27. 1 Corinthians 15:25.

Chapter 11—Enduring Hope

1. 1 Thessalonians 1:2–3.
2. James 2:18.
3. James 2:16.
4. See Mark 11.
5. Cham Dallas, "The Exclusion Zone," LeadershipU.com, http://www.leaderu.com/real/ri-intro/thezone.html (accessed December 30, 2009).
6. Matthew 25:35–36.
7. Galatians 5:6.
8. 1 Thessalonians 5:8.
9. 1 Corinthians 13:13.
10. 1 John 4:8, 16.
11. John 1:1, 14, emphasis added.
12. John 3:16.
13. Hebrews 1:1–5.
14. Hebrews 6:17–20, ESV, emphasis added.
15. Louis Talbot, *Studies in the Epistle to the Hebrews* (n.p.: n.d.), 23, quoted in Richard Phillips, *Hebrews (Reformed Expository Commentary)* (Phillipsburg, NJ: P&R Publishing), 217.
16. "We Have an Anchor" by Priscilla J. Owens. Public domain.
17. Hebrews 6:18.

Chapter 12—Abounding Hope

1. Emily Dickinson, *The Complete Poems of Emily Dickinson* (Boston, MA: Little, Brown, and Company, 1924), Part 1: Life, no. 32, http://www.bartleby.com/113/1032.html (accessed November 16, 2009).
2. The supposedly "separate but equal" policy of racial segregation and *de facto* inequality that South Africa finally dismantled in 1993.
3. Romans 15:13.

4. See Romans 5:3–5.
5. Romans 5:5.
6. Acts 14:22.
7. 2 Corinthians 4:17.
8. Augsburger, *When Enough Is Enough*, 34–35.
9. Job 23:10.
10. See Matthew 13:3–8.
11. Matthew 13:21–22.
12. See Romans 5:1–5.
13. Isaiah 40:30–31, NIV.
14. 1 Corinthians 10:11.
15. John 3:3–4.
16. John 3:7–8.
17. Isaiah 40:31, NIV.
18. Romans 5:3–5.

Chapter 13—Choosing Hope

1. Covey, *The 8th Habit*, 42.
2. Brother Andrew, *And God Changed His Mind*, 11–12.
3. Ibid., 12.
4. Ibid., 23–24.
5. Matthew 5:14.
6. Matthew 24:14, emphasis added.
7. Matthew 6:10.
8. Romans 5:17, emphasis added.
9. Covey, *The 8th Habit*, 5.
10. Ibid., 40–42.
11. Romans 15:4.
12. Covey, *The 8th Habit*, 42.
13. Ibid., 43.
14. Groopman, *The Anatomy of Hope*, 170.
15. 15. Ibid., 179.
16. Psalm 33:18.
17. Romans 12:2.
18. Phillip E. Johnson in Nancy Pearcey, *Total Truth* (Wheaton: Crossway Books, 2005), 11.
19. Ephesians 2:6.
20. Center for Reformed Theology and Apologetics, "Shorter Westminster Catechism," http://www.reformed.org/documents/index.html?mainframe=http://www.reformed.org/documents/WSC_frames.html (accessed November 17, 2009).
21. Philip Yancey, *The Jesus I Never Knew* (Grand Rapids, MI: Zondervan Publishing House, 1995), 68.
22. Charles Colson and Nancy Pearcey, *How Now Shall We Live?* (Wheaton: Tyndale House Publishers, Inc., 1999), 204–206.
23. Philip Yancey, *What's So Amazing About Grace?* (Grand Rapids, MI: Zondervan Publishing House, 1997), 110–111.

24. "Amazing Grace" by John Newton. Public domain.
25. Gerald G. May, *Addiction and Grace* (New York: Harper Collins, 1991), 20.
26. Deuteronomy 30:19–20.
27. Psalm 72:12.
28. Acts 2:21.
29. Hosea 2:15, NLT.

CHAPTER 14—THE DANCE OF HOPE

1. Charles Dickens, *A Christmas Carol*, (Public Domain Books, 2004), Amazon Kindle e-book, locations 20-28, Stave 1: Marley's Ghost.
2. Ibid., location 972, Stave IV: The Last of the Spirits.
3. Lamentations 3:22–24, ESV.
4. Philippians 4:19.
5. Hebrews 4:16.
6. Jeremiah 29:11.
7. 2 Corinthians 5:17.
8. 2 Chronicles 7:14.
9. Luke 1:37.
10. Psalm 17:8.
11. Romans 8:1.
12. Philippians 4:13.
13. Matthew 5:16.
14. Romans 8:37, NKJV.
15. 1 Peter 2:24.
16. 2 Corinthians 11:23, 30, NLT.
17. Luke 4:18–19, NLT; also see Isaiah 61:1–3.
18. Luke 24:27.
19. Luke 24:32.
20. Romans 15:4.
21. Hebrews 4:12.
22. John 1:14, NLT.
23. John 14:9.
24. The entire conversation is recorded in Luke 1:26–38, emphasis added.
25. Luke 1:38.
26. Romans 10:9.
27. Law with Gilbert, *The Power of Praise and Worship*, 276–277.
28. James 3:4–6 compares the tongue to both a rudder and a fire.
29. Romans 5:1–2.
30. Dickens, *A Christmas Carol*, location 1009.
31. Ibid., location 1010.
32. Hebrews 3:6.

WORLD COMPASSION TERRY LAW MINISTRIES

World Compassion Terry Law Ministries is a nondenominational, faith-based, international organization founded by Terry Law in 1969. For more than forty years, we have been called to work in nations where most ministers of the gospel rarely go because of political, religious, and/or economic instability, working with local bodies of believers to support the spiritual and physical transformation of lives through the loving touch of Jesus Christ.

We currently work and conduct ministry outreaches in Afghanistan, China, Iraq, Myanmar, and Iran.

Our organizational focus directs us in four strategic areas of ministry:

Church planting

Establishing local church bodies in countries where we work is our ultimate goal to provide believers an environment where they can grow spiritually, discover God's purpose in their lives, and reach more people with the message of Jesus. Through church-planting efforts we can reach the heart of these nations, bringing them the hope found only in Jesus Christ.

Training and discipleship

World Compassion is committed to providing discipleship tools so believers can grow their faith in God while learning how to tell others about the good news of Jesus Christ. We have developed and implemented in China two discipleship programs—Audio Bible Curriculum (ABC) and China Mission School (CMS). Our goal is to expand these programs to other language groups in numerous areas of the world.

Literature

One of the most powerful tools we can use to tell people about Jesus and help build their faith in Christ is the distribution of Bibles and Bible-based literature. World Compassion prints and distributes the Bible and The Story of Jesus booklet in various nations around the world. Through our online store at www.worldcompassion.tv we offer numerous teaching and preaching materials in print, CD, and DVD format.

Humanitarian outreach

It is our strategy to not only bring people the Word of God but also the compassion of God in the form of various humanitarian outreaches. Presently we are using three signature programs in target nations: Iraq Shoe Program/Shoes That Save, Afghan Women and Youth Education, and Medicine Outreach Program.

**To learn more about World Compassion
Terry Law Ministries, make a purchase from our online
store, or to give, go to our Web site:**

www.worldcompassion.tv

World Compassion
Terry Law Ministries
P. O. Box 92
Tulsa, OK 74101-0092
1.918.492.2858

World Compassion Society
P. O. Box 1415
Medicine Hat, AB T1A 7N3
Canada

World Compassion Trust
P. O. Box 777
Stourbridge, West Midlands DY8 4WZ
United Kingdom

www.worldcompassion.tv